Sally Burningham specialises in writing about health and social issues. Since the mid-1970s her main work has been as a journalist, covering news and conferences and contributing regular features to journals for doctors, social workers, therapists and administrators, as well as to publications for the general reader, especially the parenting magazines. For three years she wrote a monthly column in *Mother and Baby*. She has also written many health education booklets and reports and contributed to other publications in addition to working for a number of charities. Her first book, *Not On Your Own*, received the prestigious Medical Journalists' Association Award for the most outstanding contribution to medical journalism in 1989. *Young People Under Stress: A Parent's Guide* is being published in association with MIND.

Sally Burningham has two grown-up sons and lives in Muswell Hill in North London.

Young People Under Stress

A parent's guide

SALLY BURNINGHAM

Published by VIRAGO PRESS Limited, June 1994
42–43 Gloucester Crescent, London NW1 7PD
Copyright © Sally Burningham 1994

The right of Sally Burningham to be identified as
author of this work has been asserted by her in accordance
with the Copyright, Designs and Patents Act 1988.

*A CIP catalogue record for this book
is available from the British Library*

Typeset by M Rules
Printed in Great Britain by
Cox & Wyman Ltd, Reading, Berkshire

To Graham
with love and thanks

CONTENTS

ACKNOWLEDGEMENTS

So many individuals, including professionals, parents and young people, have given me help with this book that it would be impossible to thank them all by name. However I am immensely grateful for their generosity, their enthusiasm and their ideas.

I would like to thank Anny Brackx of MIND and Ruth Petric of Virago for asking me to write this book and for their encouragement, and Hilary Claire and Elizabeth Morton for their support.

I am also very grateful to Dr John Coleman of the Trust for the Study of Adolescence, Peter Wilson of Young Minds, and Dr Guinevere Tuffnell and Dr Richard Williams of the Royal College of Psychiatry, for their very helpful suggestions.

Finally I would like to thank both my partner and my mother for so patiently commenting on various stages of the text.

INTRODUCTION

Parents often grumble to others about their teenagers' untidy room, their strange clothes or their thoughtless behaviour. However, they may be reluctant to discuss more serious worries, should these occur, such as whether their son or daughter is depressed, acting oddly or not managing to cope. As a result, they may be unaware of just how many other parents experience similar anxieties, and feel very much alone.

Adolescence is not necessarily a particularly stressful time for all young people. Your son or daughter may encounter no more than the customary ups and downs during these years or discover their own appropriate ways of dealing with demanding situations. On the other hand, you may find that they need considerable support in overcoming problems that may be impeding their normal development or preventing them from enjoying life or functioning to the best of their ability.

This book aims to provide parents with explanations of some of the more serious kinds of problems their son or daughter may experience in adolescence, together with suggestions on ways to help the young person, and find help for themselves. It encourages parents to make the best use of the services available and of their own resources within the family or community. Relatives, friends and others close to young people may also find it helpful.

Adolescence is often thought of as a transitional period between the dependence of childhood and the responsibilities of adult life. Since each young person is an individual who develops at their own pace there is no single age at which adolescence can be said to start or finish. This book is mainly intended for parents of young people between the ages of 11 and 18. However it is important to remember that the stresses connected with adolescence may start earlier for some young people or may last well beyond the age of 18.

Adolescence can be a confusing time for parents because of the many rapid changes that are taking place, including the change in their own relationship with their son or daughter (see Part 1). You may sometimes find it difficult to decide whether the young person's moods and behaviour are simply normal reactions to everyday stresses and to new feelings and situations or signs that things are going wrong.

The fact that your daughter or son may be unwilling to confide in you because they are so anxious to preserve their privacy and independence may add to your uncertainty and even make you less sure of your own role as a parent. Although you still feel responsible for their health and well-being, you now have to think more carefully about when to step back and when to intervene. Sometimes it may feel as though you can never get it right.

Unfortunately there are no clear guidelines on when to leave a young person to manage on their own and when to offer help and parents often have to trust their own intuition. It is the persistence of odd behaviour over a period of time, the degree of distress, or the fact that your son or daughter is not coping with certain areas of their life which may indicate to you that some help is needed. Often it is the combination of a number of things which somehow don't seem quite right and which seem to be occurring increasingly frequently that may give you the clue.

Most difficulties for which a young person needs help will be quite complex and there will usually be a number of contributory factors, not all of which are easily identifiable. However, in some cases, it may be clear that a specific stress or situation is very obviously contributing to their distress. Offering help in that area may sometimes give the young person enough confidence to deal with other problems themselves (see Part 2).

2

In other instances, the young person's responses to difficulties have become so much a part of themselves, affecting much of the way that they think or react, that simply finding ways to help them deal with various outside stresses is unlikely to be sufficient. A variety of approaches may be needed. Problems that become entrenched in this way, and which may range from mild to severe, are sometimes referred to by professionals as mental health problems (see Part 3). However, your son or daughter's difficulties are unlikely to fit into neat categories and there are no hard and fast rules about classifying problems. It is far more important to ensure that the young person receives appropriate help.

Parents will often ask themselves why their particular son or daughter should experience certain problems. They may be even more puzzled if brothers and sisters, with a similar upbringing, remain unaffected. In most cases the reasons will remain unclear but it is important to remember that each young person differs in terms of their physical constitution, their temperament, the way their personality has developed and the way they interpret and make use of experience.

It may be that some young people are born more vulnerable to certain types of stress or become so at some point in their development, or that difficulties in childhood that you hoped they would grow out of surface again in adolescence, or that a combination of circumstances at a specific time simply proves too much for them to handle.

The more information you can get about your son or daughter's problem and the sooner you can persuade them to seek appropriate help the better (see Part 5). However, you may find that they are unwilling to admit that anything is wrong or to accept the help that is offered. Keep trying in a tactful way and if they are unenthusiastic about what you suggest, look for possible alternatives. They may suddenly agree that they do need help at a time when you least expect it.

Sometimes there may seem to be no way forward, but your son

or daughter still needs to know that you care about them and will give them what support you can. Whatever happens, make sure you get support for yourself and advice on how best to handle the situation (see Part 4).

Parents should not feel that they ought to be perfect or that they must get it right as far as the young person is concerned. However, your son or daughter does need to know that you are there if they need you. Never close the door in the young person's face however impossible the situation seems. No one else will care as much about their well-being or fight as persistently for their rights. You are the best resource your son or daughter has, even if they cannot always see it that way at present.

PART I

The adolescent years

CHAPTER I
Growing up

Although young people are all very different from each other, most will share certain concerns. They will want to try and make sense of who they are as separate individuals; they will want to find a group of people outside the family with whom they feel comfortable, and they will want to discover for themselves what interests them and what they enjoy. During these years your son and daughter will probably be exploring their capacity to make relationships and they may well worry about what the future holds for them in terms of satisfying employment. As at other times in life, they will want to feel valued and appreciated and to know that there are people they care about and who care about them.

Each young person changes and develops during adolescence at their own rate and in their own way. You may find that your son or daughter seems quite grown up in dealing with certain aspects of their life, but not in others, or that it is an up-and-down process. Young people often find it less stressful if they can concentrate on learning to handle changes in one or two areas at a time rather than trying to cope with too many new experiences at once. As long as they are developing and gradually becoming more mature in some areas, there is probably no need to worry. They can always deal with other areas later.

Parents, however, do need to be concerned if the young person seems stuck and reluctant to leave childhood behind in most areas, or if they can only handle changes in ways that seem self-destructive or cause a great deal of distress. In such instances it is important that the young person receives appropriate help in adjusting to the changes that are crucial in growing up.

Parents and young people are often confused as to what being an adult really means, and even the law provides very little guidance. For example, young people are free to leave school or get married when they are 16, but cannot drive till they are 17 or vote until their eighteenth birthday. Moreover, with protracted education and training and widespread unemployment, many young people remain dependent on their parents or the state for even longer, unable to take on all the responsibilities that might help them to feel that they were really grown up, should they wish.

Becoming grown up is a gradual process and there is not usually a single recognisable point when it occurs. Perhaps it is helpful to think of the years between 11 and 18 as a time when many young people can start to adjust to new experiences, gain in confidence and gradually take on more responsibility for themselves. Such a process may well continue into their twenties, depending on individual circumstances. Those who have had to cope with mental health problems or severe stress are likely to take longer to grow up as it may take them some time to catch up.

CHANGES
Physical
The most obvious changes that occur in adolescence are the numerous physical changes associated with puberty and the growth spurt, which are spread over several years. There is wide variation among young people as to when such changes begin, the order in which they happen and the length of time they take to complete.

The age at which your son or daughter starts puberty or the growth spurt will not affect their long-term physical development. However, young people, especially girls who do develop quite early, may need extra support from parents as they may look far more grown up than they really are and find it hard to cope with other people's expectations. Similarly, those who commence puberty and their growth spurt several years after the majority may need reassurance as they may feel left behind for a time.

Your daughter or son may well feel unsettled and wonder what kind of person they really are as they try to adjust to rapid alterations in their height, weight and other features, as well as in the shape of their body and the way it functions. Girls may become acutely conscious of their developing breasts and widening hips, for example; boys of their sudden increase in height and muscularity, their voice breaking or their facial hair. Both may at different times regard these changes with pleasure or embarrassment. As well as more obvious developments, there will be a rapid increase in the size of both heart and lungs, leading to greater physical strength and endurance, especially for boys.

This is a time when your son or daughter will be particularly sensitive about the way they look and very concerned about how they appear to the outside world. They are likely to spend hours in front of the mirror, often worrying about how they can possibly meet the high standards set by the media and their peers. Try to reassure them about how nice they look whenever you can. It is also important to avoid teasing them about changes that occur, or any awkwardness or clumsiness, as this is likely to make them feel even more anxious and self-conscious. Your son or daughter's preoccupation with their physical appearance is not usually vanity at this particular stage; it is a normal part of growing up.

During adolescence young people will need to come to terms with their gradual sexual maturity and the fact that they are able to reproduce, often long before they are emotionally ready for such a responsibility. As in other areas, there are great differences between young people in the way that they experience and deal with their own sexuality and increasing sexual drive. For some young people it becomes a central concern; for others it may have less importance or may assume greater importance as they get older.

Thinking

It is also apparent that during the adolescent years most young people gradually become more capable of thinking about issues in an abstract way. You may find that your son or daughter is more able to examine problems from a variety of viewpoints than when they were younger, or is more able to compare the possible consequences of several alternative actions, weighing up advantages and disadvantages in their head. In addition they may increasingly begin to question previously accepted assumptions as part of learning to think more for themselves. As a result they may go through an intensely irritating phase during which your every casual remark is subject to scrutiny or ridicule.

During adolescence young people often become more introspective. This means that they are more able to stand outside themselves and look critically at their own actions. It also means that they are likely to become more involved in examining their own thoughts and feelings and in going over and over what is happening in their lives, either on their own or in discussion with friends. You may feel impatient because your son or daughter seems for a time to be so self-centred and preoccupied with themselves. However, it is important to remember that they may be experiencing many new thoughts and feelings and that they need time to absorb these and adjust.

Emotions

Although some people do seem to have a more even temperament than others, most people expect some ups and downs in mood throughout their lives. However, many young people do experience an increased number of mood changes during adolescence, often veering from feeling rather low to fairly happy in a short space of time. This may be partly due to the physical changes that are taking place, but there may be other contributory factors such as the stresses involved in coping with new experiences. Most parents accept that a certain amount of moodiness in adolescence is normal. However, if your son or daughter's mood changes are very extreme, or if they seem unhappy for much of the time, or if they are not enjoying themselves at all even if they seem to be coping, then it is likely that some help will be needed.

During adolescence quite intense feelings often occur for the first time and some young people may have difficulties in handling them. For example, they may feel lost or lacking in direction, or they may feel acutely lonely at times, or as though they do not fit in. They may feel deep disappointment at failing to achieve what they had set out to do, they may develop a 'crush' or fall in love, or they may feel devastated at the break-up of a relationship. Although such emotions may all be part of growing up, they are none the less real and it is important that parents take them seriously and offer understanding and support if the young person does confide in them. Young people will vary the way they handle such emotions. However, if their distress seems out of all proportion to what has occurred or lasts for considerably longer than you might expect, this may well be a sign that your son or daughter is not really coping and that more help is needed.

School

One of the changes that most young people will undergo during this time is the move to a larger, and probably more anonymous, secondary school. They will need to get used to new surroundings, new classmates, and new subjects, as well as to a relationship with numerous members of staff who may not know them very well, rather than with one or two teachers as at their previous school. Some young people may find older pupils intimidating or may feel confused by the different rules. Whatever the situation, it is likely to take your son or daughter a little while to settle down and find their feet and you may need to show extra understanding during the first few months. Do not hesitate to get in touch with the school if there do seem to be any difficulties that your child is unable to deal with themselves: it will be much easier to sort out any problems at an early stage.

During their school years the young person will find that they are increasingly faced with decisions that only they can take, such as how much time to spend on study and how much to allot to friends and other activities. It is often hard for parents if they feel that their son or daughter is jeopardising their future chances by not working hard enough, but nagging is likely to be counterproductive. You can try talking calmly to them when they are in a sensible mood and showing an interest in their work, if they will let you, although in the end you will have to accept it is up to them. But be alert if your son or daughter's schoolwork has started to deteriorate for no apparent reason: this could be a sign of other problems for which they may need help.

Social life

Young people usually want to spend more time with people of their own age and less with their families during adolescence. This is a quite normal development and no reflection on parents. It is likely that relationships with the family will still remain very important for your daughter or son, even though it may not always seem so at times. You may feel a little sad at the change at first and you may need to remind yourself that it is the warm supportive relationships within the family that so often help the young person to form good relationships outside. As your son or daughter gets older you will probably feel closer to them again in a different way.

Most young people enjoy the company of friends and being with people of their own age will give them the opportunity to practise the give and take in relationships which is such an important part of growing up. In addition young people often support each other in learning to deal with new situations and with problems that arise. If your son or daughter finds it hard to make friends they may miss out on these kinds of experience. You will need to look for ways of building up their confidence so that they will find it easier to mix.

New roles

As your son or daughter get older they may assume new roles which in turn will help in growing up. They may be given more responsibility at home or school, for example, or they may play sports for a team or take part in an orchestra. They may have close friends to whom they feel a commitment. They may take on weekend or holiday jobs or full-time employment. If they stay on at school or college after the age of 16 they may find that they are treated more as an adult and expected to assume greater responsibility for organising their day. However, sometimes demands on their time may conflict, or pressures may seem too great. They may need support in sorting out what is most important for them at this stage.

Independence

One of the most important changes that normally takes place in adolescence is a change in the young person's relationship with their parents. Your son or daughter will be seeking to assert their independence and to become a person in their own right. However, they may sometimes be confused about how quickly they really want to grow up, and you yourself will still feel responsible for ensuring their well-being and safety.

It will help if you can adopt a more flexible approach than when they were younger, while at the same time making it clear that there are certain firm boundaries. In fact you will probably find that most differences arise over matters such as dress, times of coming home, household chores, homework and lack of consideration for others – the very issues over which you probably argued with your parents, and they with theirs.

However, adolescence is also a time when young people are more likely to experiment and there are probably more pressures on young people now than there were even twenty years ago. You may, quite naturally, worry about the risks they may run, especially as some of these may be outside your own experience. Your son or daughter is far more likely to take notice of your point of view if it is based on accurate information and if you are able to talk calmly and listen to what they have to say. Simply forbidding certain activities may push them into experimentation.

Young people often veer between seemingly adult attitudes one moment and childish demands the next. Sometimes they may appear to be testing you to the limits and interpreting your concern as interference; at others they may be grumbling that you do not take enough interest in their life. Such behaviour may confirm your belief that they are not yet ready for the independence they claim. However, what is important is that your son or daughter can gradually explore ways of becoming independent, without having to take responsibility in all areas. They also need to know that they have the support of family and friends if they do make mistakes.

Young people need more privacy in adolescence in order to come to terms with the changes that are taking place and in order to gradually assert their independence. You may find that your son or daughter wants to spend time in their room on their own, or is reluctant to disclose too much about their friends or activities. Try to respect their need for privacy, which is a vital part of growing up, while at the same time remaining aware of what is generally going on in their life. Give your daughter or son plenty of opportunities to be with you and talk if they wish, but don't expect them to tell you everything. Showing an interest in what they are doing, making their friends welcome, and keeping in touch with their school are probably better ways of keeping an eye on them than cross-questioning them, which they may well resent.

Nevertheless, you do need to be concerned if they spend too

long on their own, reluctantly joining you for meals or rarely seeing friends, or if there are indications that they may be involved in
risky or self-destructive activities. If your son or daughter is
unwilling to talk, get advice for yourself on what to do (see
Part 5).

Sometimes your son or daughter may find it quite hard to
handle the pressures involved in growing up. As a result they may
be rude or hurtful to you as a way of venting their angry feelings.
They may also adopt a very patronising or provoking attitude for
a time since if they can convince themselves that you are boring or
stupid, it may make it easier for them to start to break away.
This is usually just a phase that many young people go through so
try not to get too upset or to take their remarks personally. They
usually stem more from anxieties about their own development
rather than from any real criticism of you. However, if their anger
is very extreme, or if the situation does not improve as they get
older, some outside help may be needed.

You may have mixed feelings yourself about letting go and
encouraging you son or daughter's independence. After all, you
have probably invested a great deal of time and energy in their
upbringing, as well as many of your own hopes. Although you
may be relieved when you start to see them behave in a more
adult way, it can sometimes also feel like a loss, particularly if
things do not turn out exactly as you had expected. This may be
the time when you need to remind yourself that you matter too.
You may want to take the opportunity to pursue new interests, to
take on more satisfying work or simply to spend more time doing
things you enjoy.

Achieving independence is a gradual process but you should
hope that your son or daughter will increasingly take on more
responsibility for themselves and eventually develop a relationship with you that is less dependent and more reciprocal. Young
people under considerable stress or coping with mental health
problems may remain more dependent for longer, but you should
encourage as much independence as you can (see Chapter 8).

Communication

It is very important that you make time just to be with your son or daughter during adolescence so that you can talk in a relaxed and general way. If they are in the habit of talking to you, they are likely to find it far easier to come to you if they have any difficulties. Of course at times you may feel exasperated or as though you are not getting through. But try to be patient. Your daughter or son may quite often decide that they want to talk when you least expect it.

Young people often complain that parents do not really listen to what they have to say and that they frequently interrupt before they have time to finish. It is important to give your son or daughter your full attention when they are talking; they are unlikely to respond unless they feel that you are trying to understand their point of view and that you respect their opinions. If you try to put them down or start to lecture them they may well stop listening. However, this does not mean that you should not be open about your own views. Your son or daughter will probably be relieved to know that you have certain values and principles and will stand by them, when so much in their own life is constantly changing.

Young people also need to feel their wishes are listened to and taken into account when decisions are being made which affect them now or in the future. Rather than taking decisions over their head, it is important to sit down with your son or daughter and calmly talk things through. This often enables both parents and young people to see the situation from different points of view. If the young person feels their opinion is valued you are more likely to reach a compromise acceptable to everyone. Moreover, if you can show that you are prepared to be flexible over less important matters, for example, then they are more likely to respect your firm stance on matters of health and safety.

Parents who always take decisions on behalf of their son or daughter may find that the young person is less able to think for themselves when necessary or behave in an appropriately mature way. Moreover, the fact that they have not been consulted may make them more inclined to rebel or go behind their parents' backs. On the other hand, parents who simply tell their son or daughter to do whatever they want, may be giving the message that they do not really care. Most children want to know what their parents feel, at least about important issues, and they usually appreciate some support and guidance, even though they may make up their own mind in the end.

Parents need to be aware that young people may often take what they say very literally at this stage in their development. Although you may feel quite strong emotions at times such as anger, hurt or disappointment, try to focus on your son or daughter's behaviour rather than on the young person themselves. It is quite reasonable to say, 'I am very angry that you didn't let me know where you were as I was worried about your safety,' for example. Learning to consider others is part of growing up. However labelling your son or daughter as 'totally irresponsible' may make them feel that there is no point in trying, since you have such a low opinion of them anyway. It may also help if you can avoid remarks such as, 'You're on your own now', or, 'You're old enough to sort out your own problems', even if these are said lightly; your son or daughter may well take you seriously.

It is also important to realise that your daughter or son may need you to spell out certain things for them, such as the fact that you are always there to listen to any problems. Although you might think that you are simply stating the obvious, you have to remember that the young person does not have your experience and may not understand the feelings involved in being a parent. Young people need to be told how much you love them and how important they are to you, while they are growing up. They may wonder if you still feel the same about them as you did when they were younger, especially if they have been going through a difficult phase.

You will also need to stress that they should always come to you if they are in any trouble and that even if you are angry at the time, you will always stand by them. Otherwise they may not be sure of your reactions, particularly if problems have arisen because they have ignored your advice.

If you suspect that your daughter or son is having difficulties try to find a way of tactfully asking whether anything is wrong. Let them know that you are there if they need you. If they do want to talk, make sure that you have time to really listen. Don't interrupt unnecessarily or feel that you have to make judgements or provide solutions. Just being able to talk, and knowing that you are there, is likely to be a help. Show your son or daughter that you care about them in whatever way seems most appropriate. A hug can often be a great comfort for you both. Sometimes support and commonsense suggestions from you and other members of the family, and perhaps from friends, may be enough to enable your son or daughter to cope.

However, in some instances further help may be needed. You are far more likely to be able to persuade your son or daughter to accept some sort of help if you are aware of just what is available (see Part 5). Depending on your son or daughter's difficulty there may be a variety of approaches, ranging from help offered by professionals and voluntary organisations to support available within your own community. However, if your son or daughter is unwilling to accept help at present, you should not feel that you and your family have to struggle to support the young person on your own. Get advice and support for yourselves at an early stage. Otherwise the stress may become too great.

PART 2

Stresses
and reactions

The adolescent years are not necessarily more difficult than other periods of life. However, they are a time when the young person has to cope with many changes, with new situations and with learning to make more decisions for themselves. They will be less able than older people to draw on previous experience both in terms of understanding their own feelings and in coping with problems that may arise. This means that reassurance and support from family and friends will be particularly crucial at this time.

Most young people will have many of the same anxieties you probably had yourself as an adolescent. They will worry about their appearance, about friends and relationships, about their family, about schoolwork and about their future, for example. But as each person is an individual and each set of circumstances unique, your daughter or son may also experience quite different stresses from the ones you or their brothers or sisters encountered, or react to them in a quite different way.

It may become apparent that what was a worry for you or other members of the family is not of great concern for them, while situations that you all handled without much trouble may present problems. Moreover, what may be perceived as encouragement or stimulation by one young person may be experienced as pressure by another. It is also important to remember that stresses are usually much harder for young people to handle if several occur at the same time or in close succession, if they occur against a background of family problems or if future prospects seem bleak due to unemployment, for example.

You also need to be aware that your son or daughter may experience certain pressures such as the need to succeed at school or gain qualifications, or the demand to behave in a way that is acceptable to their peers, at an earlier age than you yourself experienced them. If such pressures occur before they feel ready to handle them, they may well feel very stressed. Conflicting pressures or conflicting expectations from parents, teachers, peers or the media, for example, are also stressful to deal with, particularly if they are encountered at an age when the young person has not yet really decided what they want for themselves.

You cannot protect your son or daughter from all forms of stress. Indeed, learning to cope with certain adverse experiences is part of growing up. Moreover they may not always confide in you if they are having difficulties. But you can make sure they know you are there to provide support and you can offer them opportunities to talk if they wish. Young people who are coping with changes and new situations need a safe place to which they can retreat where not too much is expected of them. You can try to make sure that you provide this comforting environment at home, particularly when you know they are under stress.

You can also try not to get too irritated if your son or daughter switches from highly assertive and independent behaviour one moment to dependent childish behaviour the next. However infuriating for you, this is a normal part of growing up and may well serve as a safety valve for the young person who suddenly feels they cannot cope with any more stress.

Some stresses may be inevitable, but others may be avoidable. It is important for parents to look at the pressures they may be exerting on their son or daughter, perhaps without realising what they are doing. It is also important to consider the pressures the young person may be putting on themselves in order to fulfil what they see as their parent's expectations, whether these are to succeed at school or to have a certain range of interests or experiences, for example.

Parents quite naturally invest a great deal in their children, often wanting them to enjoy activities that they themselves missed out on or even to achieve what they themselves were unable to manage. However, it is crucial for parents to step back and see their children as people in their own right and to encourage them to find out what they want for themselves in life.

It seems that although sensible encouragement by parents to achieve realistic goals will often contribute to a young person's sense of self-esteem, high levels of pressure from parents to succeed may often actually reduce their confidence. Parents therefore have the difficult task of finding a way of showing concern and interest in their child's progress without exerting too much pressure and thereby adding to their stress.

If your daughter or son does seem anxious about any aspect of their studies or other activities try and get across that what they are doing should be for their own interest, benefit or enjoyment and not to please you or anyone else. If they have set their heart on a particular achievement try not to identify too much with this or they may worry about letting you down. Try to encourage them to keep their options open, to work steadily at their own pace and not to regard setbacks as disasters. Of course you will want to show you are delighted by any successes, but it is important that they know you still love and value them just as much if they fail or make mistakes.

Each young person may have different capacities to cope with varying sorts of stress, depending on the circumstances and their own personality. However, nearly all young people will find it easier if they only have to cope with one difficulty at a time. Many do seem to know this unconsciously and often tackle the different issues involved in growing up at different times during adolescence and at their own pace. Young people who are forced to cope with more than one challenge at once, perhaps because physical changes have occurred later and coincided with increased demands at school or from peers, for example, may need extra understanding and support.

If you know or suspect that your son or daughter is troubled or stressed, then the best form of support you can offer is to be available if they wish to talk. Just talking and knowing that you understand may give your son or daughter a sense of relief. Putting your arm round the young person, or giving them a hug, if appropriate, may be reassuring for you both. If you have had similar feelings or experiences at some time yourself, you may wish to tell them to help them feel less alone, but avoid going into detail unless they ask. It is far more important to listen to what they have to say themselves.

Don't feel you always have to offer solutions. However, if your son or daughter wants to discuss what they should do, you may find that looking at the situation in detail and at just what upsets them, will give you both some ideas on what could be changed. If the young person is distressed about an issue about which you have little knowledge or experience, then getting as much information as you can and talking to relevant professionals, voluntary organisations or other parents, while still preserving confidence, may enable you to offer more appropriate help.

If your son or daughter does seem anxious or stressed you may be able to help by trying to ensure, in a tactful way, that they lead a reasonably balanced life. For example, if they are studying very hard you will probably want to persuade them to leave time for relaxation and enjoyment; if they rarely go out you will want to look for ways of helping them to improve their social life; and if their confidence is low you may want to suggest that they take up a new interest.

Regular exercise can be an effective way of preventing the build-up of stress. Moreover, if the young person is fit they are likely to have more energy to cope. It is also important to keep an eye on what your son or daughter eats: too little food or a poorly balanced diet can add to feelings of tension, as well as being bad for their health. Regular family meals are a good way of ensuring that your son or daughter is eating sensibly. They are also a helpful means of ensuring that members of the family really are communicating with each other and aware of what is going on so that they are able to offer support, if necessary. It may help everyone if you can make sure that you all eat together in a relaxed way at least two or three times a week.

Young people often look so grown up and seem so self-assured that parents may be unaware just how unsure of themselves they really are. Your son or daughter is quite likely to go through a stage of wondering why anyone should like them, even if they appear to have plenty of friends, or of believing that they are stupid, despite the fact that they may be doing well at school. Look for things to praise such as personal qualities that will help your son or daughter feel good about themselves. Telling them how nice they look when they go out can often help to boost their confidence.

This part of the book looks at just some of the stresses young people may experience, some of the circumstances in which stresses may occur and possible reactions. It is by no means comprehensive. As a parent you need to be aware of possible areas of stress for your daughter or son and to be particularly vigilant if the stresses are severe or if the young person is trying to cope with several stresses close together or at the same time. Make sure they know you are always available to listen and offer support. Do not hesitate to suggest outside help if you feel it is needed. If your son or daughter will not go for help, get help for yourself.

CHAPTER 2

Possible Problems

ADOPTION

If you have adopted your son or daughter at an early age you may well find that they become more curious about their origins in adolescence and want to discover more about their birth parents. It is important to take this seriously and make opportunities to talk through feelings about adoption and any issues involved.

Sometimes in the normal adolescent process of rejecting your values, they may imagine how their birth parents might be different and may try to identify with them or even taunt you with the fact that you are not their 'real' parents. Try not to retaliate, however hurt you feel. Remember that they are struggling with their own questions of identity, which are normal in adolescence but which in their case have been further complicated by adoption. However, if things do become difficult ask for support from your original adoption agency or social services.

If you adopt a young person who has already suffered considerable problems before they came into your family you need to be aware that they may find it difficult to deal with what you consider to be normal family intimacy. They may feel very angry about what has happened to them in the past and direct their rage at you. It is important to remember that underneath they may in fact be very frightened, vulnerable or depressed. Look for small things to work on together and small signs of progress rather than expecting the young person to be emotionally transformed because you are offering them love and security. Make sure that you have emotional support for yourself as well as for them. In some cases family therapy or counselling may be appropriate (see Chapter 12).

BEREAVEMENT

Your son or daughter will need time to grieve after the death of someone close, whether that person was a relative or friend. They will also need support to enable them to work through their feelings and come to terms with their loss.

Young people quite often bottle up their distress for fear of upsetting others or because they think that no one will understand. They need the opportunity to explore their feelings, when they are ready, or they run the risk of developing anxiety, depression or other problems at a later stage in life, perhaps when another crisis occurs. Moreover, young people who are not given an opportunity to acknowledge their grief may react by behaving in an uncharacteristic way, perhaps becoming more distant or more aggressive and uncooperative, for example.

As a parent you need to make it clear that you are there to listen whenever they wish to talk about the person who has died or their own confused feelings. Crying can be a good way to release pent-up emotions so let them cry if they can, and cry with them if that comes naturally. There is no need to say very much; hugging your son or daughter and showing that you care will probably be more comforting.

If you are so distressed by the death yourself that you cannot offer your son or daughter the support they need, try to make sure that another relative or family friend is there for them. It is vital that your son or daughter knows that there is someone who understands their feelings and that they do not have to cope alone.

You need to know that the young person may experience a number of bewildering emotional and physical symptoms associated with grief at different times over the coming months for which they may be quite unprepared. They will need reassurance that these symptoms are quite normal reactions to a bereavement and not signs that they are going 'mad'. They may feel shock, numbness or disbelief about the death, sadness, longing for the person, anger at what has happened, or pain. They may feel guilty that they are not reacting in the expected way, that they could not prevent the death or that they themselves are still alive. Their eating and sleeping patterns may be disturbed, they may have difficulties in concentrating and they may sometimes feel exhausted, sick, shaky or unwell. However, at times they will find that they forget about the death and can concentrate on their everyday activities.

Make sure that you inform the young person's school or place of work about the bereavement so that allowances can be made and support offered. You also need to remember that it may be very important for your daughter or son to attend the funeral and to be involved in discussions about practical arrangements. You may want to exclude them in order to protect them, but to the young person it may seem as though you are denying them the right to mourn like everyone else.

If your son or daughter is unable to talk to you or their friends about their feelings, if they are withdrawing from friends or if they seem to be becoming more anxious or depressed than you would expect, you might suggest that they talk to the GP or school nurse for example (see Chapter 9), or see a counsellor or telephone the Cruse—Bereavement helpline (see Chapter 15).

BULLYING

Research shows that bullying is a major source of anxiety for many young people who are either bullied themselves or see others being bullied. Bullying may take place at school, at work, in the neighbourhood or even within the family, for example. You need to be aware of the possibility of bullying if your son or daughter seems inexplicably distressed.

Bullying may involve physical attacks, ranging from hair pulling or pinching to more violent assaults. It can also involve taunting through name calling or gestures, continual, insensitive 'teasing' or deliberately and very obviously excluding the young person from particular activities or groups. Even mild bullying can cause a great deal of suffering, especially as the young person will have neither the skills nor the experience to deal with the situation. Young people often have difficulty in telling their parents that they are being bullied, either because they are frightened or ashamed, or because they want to protect them from worrying.

The young person who is bullied is likely to feel humiliated or fearful because they have been singled out for physical attacks or for ridicule or abuse, either by one person or a group. They may also feel angry or vulnerable because their feelings have been disregarded, and anxious about future episodes and how they will cope. Their self-esteem is likely to sink and some young people may even come to believe that they deserve to be bullied. Unless adequate support is given there is the danger that they may carry their fears with them into adult life, giving rise to difficulties in relationships and other problems.

Signs that a young person is being bullied may be similar to the signs for many other sorts of difficulties so you may need to question your son or daughter very sensitively. However you may notice that they seem unwilling to go to places they once went to quite happily, or that they insist on changing their route. Or you may find that they come home with cuts and bruises or damaged possessions or that they seem to be continually losing money, which in reality is being extorted from them. There may be changes in behaviour such as not wanting to go to school or work, a loss of interest in activities, tearfulness, anxiety or depression. Some young people may resort to substance misuse as a way of handling their worries, and some may even attempt to take their own lives.

If you discover your son or daughter is being bullied it is important to take it very seriously. If you brush it aside or tell them that they should be able to handle it themselves they will feel even more isolated and afraid. They need to know that other young people have had similar experiences, that you understand just how upsetting it must be and that they are not to blame. Above all they will need reassuring that they do not have to cope with it on their own. Give your son or daughter the opportunity to express their feelings, offer them comfort and try talking through what can be done to change the situation.

Bullying thrives on secrecy so it is important to bring it out into the open and to enlist the right support. The young person may be more willing to discuss the matter with other appropriate people if you explain that unless everything possible is done to stop the bullying, others may suffer as well.

If the bullying is taking place at school the young person may be prepared to talk to a teacher they trust. It will help if you also talk to teachers yourself to make sure that they are taking the problem seriously and that it is being satisfactorily handled. Keep a check, as bullying can easily resurface. Talking to other parents may also help.

If bullying is going on within the family, perhaps under the guise of teasing, it is important that everyone within the family is clear about the situation and tries to sort it out. If you are unable to deal with it yourselves some outside help, perhaps in the form of family therapy (see Chapter 12), may be appropriate.

The young person who has been bullied will need support to help raise their confidence and self-esteem. They will also need strategies to enable them to try and prevent bullying from recurring or to deal with it if it does occur. They may discuss such strategies with family members, teachers, professionals and friends. Helpful ideas may also be available in books and leaflets on bullying. Ask at your local library. Social skills training is often very useful (see Chapter 12).

Young people who bully also need help or they may continue their behaviour as they grow older, causing problems for themselves and others. It may be a shock to discover that your son or daughter is bullying others but it is essential to deal with it as soon as possible and to try and find the reasons for their behaviour. You may discover that they have been bullied themselves and are taking it out on others or that their own sense of self-esteem is low and that bullying makes them feel more confident. Sometimes they may simply be confusing bullying behaviour with strong leadership.

Talk to your son or daughter about their actions and try to help them find more satisfactory alternatives to bullying. Look for ways to increase their sense of self-esteem. Giving them responsibilities or encouraging new interests may help them to mature and begin to consider others. Social skills training can also be very helpful (see Chapter 12).

You may need support yourself as discovering your son or daughter is being bullied or is bullying others can be very painful. Talking to friends, other parents, professionals or to someone on a helpline may give you the strength you need to help your son or daughter deal with situations in more appropriate ways (see Chapter 15).

DISABILITIES AND OTHER SPECIAL NEEDS

Young people with physical disabilities or recurrent bouts of illness often cope reasonably well during childhood. However, they may find they are under much greater stress as they struggle to adjust to all the physical, emotional and social changes which occur during adolescence. In addition, as they start to compare themselves with other young people of a similar age, as is usual in adolescence, they are likely to become more acutely aware of their own condition and the limitations it imposes. As a result they may feel angry, frustrated or distressed because it seems unfair and because they are unable to change the situation.

In their early teens your daughter or son may well be very concerned with their physical appearance and with trying to look and behave as much as possible like other admired young people of a similar age. Later, like most young people, they are likely to have anxieties about their ability to form friendships or close relationships, about how to handle their sexual and emotional needs, about social activities and about work or educational opportunities for example. However, unless a great deal of understanding and support can be given, your daughter or son's worries may be exacerbated by lack of confidence or low self-esteem arising from feelings that they are in some way 'different'. They may also find it harder to deal with new situations if they have had a very protected childhood and may need extra encouragement.

Parents should be prepared for the fact that young people may at times react angrily to their illness or disability in adolescence by behaving as if it is not part of them. They may disobey diet restrictions, for example, refuse to take drugs, fail to attend check-ups or insist that they can do exactly what their friends can do without taking any sensible precautions. At other times they may become over-dependent on advice and consult doctors over the least little difficulty. This can be a very worrying period for parents. You may need to talk through your anxieties with a professional or another parent before deciding how to handle the situation. Excessive nagging is usually counterproductive but you may have to be very firm if their health is seriously threatened.

If your child has learning difficulties you may find that they will go through the same phases as most adolescents, but that these will probably extend over a longer period. It is important to encourage them to look after themselves and to be as independent as possible. You should try and make sure that you communicate with them in a way that is appropriate to their age and that you make sure that they know that they are valued for themselves. You will need to ensure that your son or daughter understands the process of maturing physically and sexually, as they are likely to become increasingly aware of their own sexual feelings. You may need to consult with their school on how best to get such information across.

As a parent you need to be aware of the extra problems your

son or daughter may face because of their illness or disability, and the additional support they may need. Be prepared to listen and to talk through problems openly and honestly with the young person if you can, rather than pushing them aside because they are uncomfortable. You will probably need advice on how best to handle different problems as they occur from the appropriate disability organisation, from a teacher or professional who is involved with the young person, or from other parents who have children with similar needs. Some young people may benefit from individual counselling or from group discussions (see Chapter 12). However, if your son or daughter shows signs of depression, anxiety or other mental health difficulties you should not assume that this is simply their way of reacting to their disability. Most mental health problems have a mixture of causes and you should seek appropriate help just as you would for a young person without these special needs.

DISRUPTIVE BEHAVIOUR

Young people may behave in an antisocial way for a variety of reasons. Isolated incidents or short-lived phases of fighting, stealing, destruction of property or misbehaviour at school are quite common, especially in early adolescence, and may be due to peer pressure, boredom or rebellion. Parents need to listen to the young person and to try and find the reasons for their behaviour.

When talking to your son or daughter it is important to remain very firm and steady about where you stand and what you believe. It may help if you can discuss calmly how such actions affect other people's lives and look together at alternative and less destructive ways of dealing with situations. Try not to get too angry or appear too shocked as this may push the young person into continuing such behaviour. If you are worried that your daughter or son may be breaking the law you could ask for advice, anonymously if you wish, from the duty officer at your local social services or probation service (see Chapter 15).

However, some young people may express their distress, or their inability to cope, through repeated antisocial behaviour. Such difficulties often surface after the change to a secondary school where the child may fail to keep up with work or make close friends. As a result they may rapidly lose confidence, thus adding further to their distress, which may then show itself through unmanageable behaviour either at home or school, or through antisocial activities in the community.

Parents need to seek help at an early stage where possible before such behaviours become entrenched and before the young person acquires the label of a troublemaker which may be hard to shake off. They need to try and work with the school and with other relevant professionals to try and find the reasons for their son or daughter's distress, to help raise their self-esteem and to provide them with strategies to cope in a more appropriate way. Social skills training may be helpful (see Chapter 12).

Some young people express their feeling through violence which is often directed at parents. This lack of control can be frightening for parents as well as for the young person themselves. You may feel very ashamed if your son or daughter is violent but it is important to get support, whether from a professional, a helpline or an understanding friend, so that you can try and help the young person deal with their reactions before these become a habit.

It may help to look at how you communicate with your son or daughter and to find ways to avoid provoking them and remaining calm. Whatever you do, avoid retaliating either physically or verbally, as the tension will then escalate. If an explosion seems imminent try to walk away and do something to soothe yourself until things have quietened down. At that point you might be able to sit down very calmly and discuss the situation and listen to what is upsetting them. Family therapy, counselling or social skills training may all be helpful (see Chapter 12). Violence is also sometimes associated with a mental health difficulty for which help will be needed.

FAMILY PROBLEMS

Family problems are quite often a source of stress for young people, especially if they are not openly discussed. Such problems may include tension or conflict, worries over money or employment, illness or disability, or the effects of drink or depression on someone in the family. Your son or daughter may not mention their concern because they do not want to add to your worries or because they are uncertain about just what is going on. However, they may show their anxieties through changes in behaviour such as going out all the time, remaining in their room or trying to take over too many family responsibilities. You may also notice a decline in schoolwork or that they have become more aggressive, uncooperative, anxious, sad or withdrawn, for example.

Most families have to deal with problems at one time or another and the more open you can be with young people, the more you will enable them to cope. In the long term it may be less distressing for your son or daughter to deal with the actual situation, however upsetting, with your support, than to feel that they cannot trust you to tell them the truth. Moreover, unless they have information about a specific problem they may imagine that things are worse than they are, or that they themselves are in some way to blame, or even that you no longer care about them because you are always so short tempered or preoccupied. It can come as a great relief to understand the real reasons for your worry and to know that you still love them just as much. But don't be surprised if your son or daughter appears angry or uninterested at first. They may need time to absorb the new information.

As a parent you may feel you are stretched to your utmost in trying to cope with a particular problem but it is important to put time aside to explain the situation in a way that is appropriate to the young person's age and development without apportioning blame and without dwelling too much on personal details. Make sure that you listen to what your son or daughter has to say and that you give them the opportunity to express their feelings. It is often hard to take in upsetting information, so several discussions may be needed or you may want to talk again as the situation changes. You may be very touched to find that your son or daughter is able to offer you emotional or practical support, but be careful not to offload too much on to their shoulders and don't be hurt if this support doesn't last or is only available in patches. Swinging from mature to more childish dependent behaviour is part of growing up.

You may also find you are more stressed if your children's adolescence coincides with a difficult stage in life for you. It may simply be that you feel you have less energy than when you were younger or you may be embarking on a new career or on a training which is more demanding than you had anticipated. Perhaps you had been looking forward to greater freedom once your children became more independent, only to find that elderly parents are demanding increasing attention. You may find that you or your partner are forced to face early retirement or unemployment or you may just feel disappointed that you have achieved less than you had hoped in your working life. Or it may be that your relationship with your partner is going through a sticky patch or that as a single parent you are feeling particularly lonely or isolated. At such times you may feel impatient with some of the less reasonable claims on your attention that your son or daughter may make. Nevertheless, it is important that the young person knows that you are always there if they really need you and that you try to put time aside just to be with them.

Continual tension or arguments within the family, for whatever reason, will be a source of considerable anxiety and stress for your son or daughter, especially if they feel pushed into taking sides or trying to smooth things over. If the difficulties are between you and your partner, it may help if you can make time together, away from the family, to try and sort things out. If the problems involve other members of the family, then sitting down together and attempting to listen calmly to each person's point of view may help. However, it is not easy to resolve differences on your own, particularly if they are complex or have built up over a considerable period, and you may need some outside help whether from a relative or trusted friend or a professional or voluntary agency.

You will almost certainly also need some help if either you or your partner are using violence to express your feelings. Not only will you be contributing to an atmosphere of fear within the family, you will also be giving a message to young people that this is an acceptable way of resolving conflict. If you find that you are hitting your partner or your son or daughter, try and work out what triggers your reactions. Then look for ways of preventing yourself from becoming too stressed such as having a bath, going for a walk or just spending a little time on your own. Avoid alcohol at these times as it will make you feel less inhibited and more inclined to lash out. It may help if you and your partner talk to someone you both trust or you may need some counselling to understand what is making you feel so angry and to find more appropriate ways of showing your emotions.

If one parent is affected by a serious or long-term physical illness or by a mental health problem there is still much that the other parent can do to protect young people from excessive stress, either by making time to be with them and give them attention, or by making sure that another trusted adult in whom they can confide, such as a grandparent, is available.

Similarly it is important to make sure that time and support are available for the brothers and sisters of a young person with an illness, disability or mental health problem. It is crucial that brothers and sisters do not feel that they have to bottle up their feelings or that their needs take second place.

It is likely that your relationship with your partner, if you have one, will come under considerable strain if your son or daughter is experiencing problems, and this in turn will affect the rest of the family. You may feel very tense and preoccupied but it is important to try and make some time to relax with your partner and to consider each other's needs. Accept any offers of help from friends or relatives to look after your children, for example, so that you can go out for an evening together, or even just for a walk. If you can have some time to enjoy being together, you will probably find you have more energy to cope.

If you are a lone parent you may feel particularly vulnerable if one of your children is experiencing difficulties. This may be partly because there is no one else to fully share the responsibility and partly because thoughtless people, with very little evidence, will often blame the young person's problems on the fact that you are bringing them up on your own. This can be particularly hurtful when you are struggling to do the best you can, often in difficult circumstances, and have invested a great deal of time and love in your relationship with your child. It is important that you get support for yourself either from family and friends, from professionals or helpful organisations such as Gingerbread, so that you can draw on the strengths you have in order to cope with the situation in a positive way (see Chapter 15).

If you yourself are suffering from a mental health difficulty such as depression, or drinking too much, for example, then getting support and help for yourself is probably the best way to help your family. Young people who are forced to grow up too soon and take on too much responsibility for their parents are often vulnerable themselves to anxiety and depression both at the time and in later years.

If there are problems affecting the family which you are unable to deal with among yourselves, then some outside help may be needed. Depending on the difficulty, marital therapy, family therapy or advice from a professional or from a voluntary organisation, or from someone you trust, for example, may be appropriate (see Part 5). Even if other members of the family are unwilling to seek help, get support for yourself to help you find more appropriate ways to deal with the situation.

FOSTER CARE

You may be providing foster care for a teenager in your own home in order to give the young person and their family time to sort out their problems or to help the young person to learn to live independently. You will not be trying to take the place of a parent, since most young people have parents of their own, although you will be trying to establish a relationship with the young person as a consistent and caring adult whom they can trust. This will include providing good basic physical care, setting reasonable limits on behaviour and trying to build up their confidence and self-esteem.

Young people who come into foster care are often under considerable stress. In addition to the normal ups and downs of adolescence they may well have been anxious for a long time because their parents were finding it increasingly difficult to cope, perhaps because of illness or other difficulties; or they may have undergone very distressing experiences such as sexual or physical abuse. In addition they will miss their familiar surroundings and may be ashamed of being in foster care.

You will want to discuss any problems that may arise with the social worker, especially if the young person seems anxious or depressed or is behaving in an odd or unpredictable way. You will need preparation, training and help in order to support the young person. Contact the National Foster Care Association for information and advice (see Chapter 15).

FRIENDSHIP AND PEER GROUPS

Close friendships and acceptance by a wider circle of their contemporaries become increasingly important for most young people during early adolescence. Your son or daughter is likely to start spending a great deal more time with people of their own age who are going through the same stages of development and puzzling over the same problems.

However, although they will probably be very influenced by

their peers in matters such as dress, hairstyle and choice of entertainment and are more likely to discuss everyday ups and downs with their friends, they will still need your constant support and your help and advice over major decisions affecting their future. They are far more likely to consult you if you can remain reasonably tolerant over the minor differences that are part of growing up.

Adolescence is an important time for learning social skills such as how to make friends and how to mix with people. Close friends can provide support and understanding, while being part of a wider group can give young people a sense of confidence. A young person who lacks close friends and who is not accepted by their peers is likely to find the adolescent years more stressful. They will have to cope on their own with all the problems for which other young people normally provide support, as well as with the distress of feeling unwanted or unpopular. Even those who appear to be mixing with their peers may at times feel very lonely, particularly if they have no close friends.

Some young people may be isolated because they are shy or withdrawn, because they lack the social skills to make friends, or because they seem in some way different. Encouraging out-of-school interests may be one way to build up their confidence and help them to make friends. If your daughter or son has gradually become more reclusive because they are studying hard, you may need to tactfully encourage them to go out with friends and relax or tensions may build up. Distancing oneself from friends may also be one of the signs of a mental health problem such as depression for which help will be needed. If you are worried about your son or daughter's lack of friends or loneliness it may help to talk through their difficulties with a professional, a voluntary organisation or someone you trust who could advise you on ways to help (see Part 5).

Of course, pressure from peers to conform can be a problem for many young people. In early adolescence in particular, there may be pressures for boys to appear tough or girls to show that they are attractive. Parents do need to understand that it is often hard for young people to resist peer pressure since if they do it may mean that in future they will be excluded from the group. However, they are far more likely to be able to say 'no' to unwanted pressure if they know they have their family's understanding and support. Close friends can also help young people resist unwanted pressure. Older adolescents, who are more mature and confident, find it easier to resist peer pressure and make their own choices.

GAY OR LESBIAN ORIENTATION

Many parents feel very upset or shocked when they first find out that their son or daughter is strongly attracted to young people of the same sex or has embarked on a lesbian or gay relationship, especially if it is not a possibility that they have considered before. Quite often they may be surprised by the strength of their own reactions. In addition they may worry about what people may think, about the prejudices that the young person is likely to encounter and about risks such as AIDS. It is also quite normal for many parents to experience sharp regrets at the thought of not becoming grandparents. Rather than discussing such feelings with your son or daughter, who will be anxious enough about your reactions, it is important to get some support for yourself. Talking to another parent on a helpline, for example, can give you the opportunity to share your feelings with someone who has had a similar experience and work through your anxieties, so that you can maintain an open and accepting relationship with your son or daughter (see Chapter 15).

You need to remember that young people who discover that they are attracted to someone of the same sex may feel very anxious, confused and isolated. They may worry that they are different from their friends and they may try to suppress or conceal their feelings for fear of disapproval or rejection by their family or their peers or because they feel ashamed. Anxieties about their sexual orientation may begin to dominate their life, sometimes resulting in depression or other problems. However acceptance and emotional support from parents and from others who are close can make all the difference in enabling the young person to feel happy and confident about their sexual feelings and to see them as simply part of life.

It may be very difficult for your son or daughter to talk to you about this issue and they are likely to have spent a long time thinking about it first. Whether it comes as a surprise to you or not, try to listen to what the young person has to say rather than jumping in and offering advice, making judgements or overloading them with your own reactions. What is important is that the young person trusts you enough to confide their feelings and that you respond in a positive way. You may want to emphasise that developing a good and caring relationship with someone, in which they feel confident and able to be themselves, matters more than whether that person is male or female. Try to make it clear to your son or daughter that you love them and are proud of them and that nothing has changed except that you have some new information about them.

In some instances sexual attraction to someone of the same sex may turn out to be a passing phase. In others the young person may be quite certain of their sexual orientation and may need some support, for example at school, where there may be a risk of being bullied. Your daughter or son may find also it helpful to contact an organisation such as the London Lesbian and Gay Switchboard (see Chapter 15) to discuss any concerns and to find details of local lesbian and gay youth organisations.

ILLNESS OR ACCIDENT

A young person who becomes ill or incapacitated by an accident for any length of time during adolescence may worry both about their physical condition and about what they are missing in terms of work and social activity. It is important to be as open as you can about their condition and the length of time it may take them to recover or readjust. The unknown is nearly always more worrying than the known. Try to encourage friends to visit so that they do not lose touch with what is going on. In some situations you may be able to get books from school or arrange for home tuition so that your son or daughter does not drop too far behind, but only suggest this if your are quite sure that they can cope.

The body and mind are closely linked. Just as someone who is emotionally distressed is likely to experience physical symptoms such as muscle tension, for example, so someone who is unwell is likely to experience emotional symptoms and may be more anxious or depressed than usual or may seem very demanding, irritable, tearful or angry. Accept that these symptoms are caused by their physical condition and try to be patient. They will need looking after, reassuring and comforting. However, you also need to be aware that depression can follow some illnesses such as glandular fever or influenza, and that drugs prescribed for certain illnesses sometimes produce depression as a side-effect. Consult the GP if such depression occurs or if you are at all worried about your son or daughter's emotional reactions.

Parents of young people who are recovering from a lengthy or serious illness or accident should be aware that they will need some time to convalesce and readjust. You may need to reassure your son or daughter that they should take things easy and not expect to do too much at once. If they rush back immediately into activities they are likely to find it hard to cope both physically and emotionally and may become anxious or depressed. In some instances they may also be upset because it is difficult for them to catch up with work, because they have missed out on activities or because friends have moved on. They may need a great deal of understanding and support during these months. If they are still at school make sure that teachers are aware of the situation and can offer appropriate help.

PREGNANCY

If you discover that your daughter is pregnant or that your son could become a father you will almost certainly feel very shocked and upset. You may also feel angry, guilty, anxious or ashamed and perhaps even wonder where you went wrong. You will need help from family or trusted friends to enable you to come to terms with your own feelings and offer your son or daughter support in a calm and practical way.

It is important for your future relationship with your son or daughter that you try to accept what has happened as soon as possible and that you avoid being judgmental if you can. Telling the young person that they have been irresponsible or blaming them in some way will only lead to friction and make the situation even more difficult to manage. The young person may be very frightened and assurances that you still love them and think highly of them are important in helping them to retain their self-esteem.

Encourage your daughter to visit the GP as soon as possible to discuss the situation. If she, or she and her partner, wish to arrange a termination then the earlier your daughter sees the doctor the simpler this will be. If she, or she and her partner, wish to have the baby then the sooner antenatal care commences the better. You will of course have your own moral standpoint or views about what might be best in the circumstances but you will need to be very patient in order to help the young people to come to the decision that is right for them. If they decide on a termination both young people may need support and perhaps counselling for some time afterwards to deal with possible feelings of guilt or loss.

If, on the other hand, they decide to continue with the pregnancy your practical and emotional support will be essential. Young girls who have to cope with disapproval and rejection on top of the problems of pregnancy will be very vulnerable to depression and other problems. Young boys who become fathers need help in meeting their responsibilities in an appropriate way.

44

However, there is no reason why a teenager should not be just as good a parent as an older person as long as they receive plenty of support.

Young girls who are pregnant are often very unwilling to attend the clinic for antenatal care or for parentcraft classes perhaps because all the other women seem so much older and more assured. But this sort of care and instruction is vital for their own health and well-being and that of the baby. If the baby's father is unable or unwilling to accompany her you might offer to attend with your daughter or see whether an older sister or a friend would be willing to go along. There may also be organisations in your area that offer support to pregnant teenagers and young mothers. Ask at your library or citizens advice bureau. The Trust for the Study of Adolescence publishes a guide to such organisations (see Chapter 15).

It is important to talk through arrangements for looking after the baby at an early stage to avoid later resentments and stresses. Grandparents need to be clear about just what they can offer when discussing plans for the future and how you can all best give support. You also need to be careful that you do not step in and take over completely in your delight over the new baby. Your son or daughter may still seem like a child to you but they are responsible for their own child.

RACE AND CULTURE

There are many acceptable ways to bring up young people. Parents from different backgrounds or cultures, or even from the same background or culture, will have their own approaches and values and often their own particular strengths and ways of supporting young people that may assist them in growing up.

Making efforts to impart your own culture to your son or daughter can help to give them a sense of identity and raise their self-esteem. In addition, close links with your own community can provide valuable support for your family. However, you do need to be aware that young people who come from minority groups, or from backgrounds which are very different from most of the other young people around them, are likely to face stress, particularly in the adolescent years, when they will most want to resemble their contemporaries. They may feel torn between two sets of values: those of their family or community, on the one hand, and those of the majority of their contemporaries, on the other, and they may have to encounter hurtful prejudice.

Conflicting Values

If you belong to a minority group with its own strongly held values and customs you may feel very concerned about the possibility of your son or daughter deviating in any way from the standards set by your family or community. But it is important to recognise that the young person may feel very stressed by the conflicting pressures of trying to live up to your expectations while at the same time behaving in a way that is acceptable to their peers and the world around them. Moreover, the difficulties which your son or daughter will encounter as an adolescent may be very different from the ones you had to cope with, especially if you were brought up in your country of origin.

The young person is more likely to respect your views if you show that you are prepared to listen to what they have to say and if you make an effort to understand their feelings. They may well express frustration when they see that other young people are allowed more freedom of choice, for example, or feel rejected when they find that they are excluded from friends' conversations because they are not able to join in their social activities.

Of course there will be certain values that are fundamental to your religion or culture and you will want to stand firm on these, but there may be other aspects where you could bend a little in order to make it easier for your son or daughter to cope with life in the world as it is today. You may even find that you are clinging to certain traditions of your own childhood while things have moved on in your country of origin and views are now less strict.

It may seem that your son or daughter is being very disrespect-ful if they question your authority or want to discuss your decisions, but try not to react in an angry way. Remember that questioning is a normal part of adolescent development and one that you yourself probably went through. If you can use the opportunity to discuss any problems in a calm and reasonable manner, the young person will be less likely to misbehave or feel the need to go behind your back. If you do issue threats or ulti-matums and the young person disobeys you on a minor point, they may then feel that they cannot come to you if they are really in trouble. Try not to see any odd lapses on your son or daugh-ter's part as a total rejection of you and your culture. However hurt you may feel, keep talking to them and keep the door open or you may push them into more extreme behaviour. What they want for themselves as young adults may not be so very different from what you want for them, so try to be patient and under-standing.

Prejudice

Facing discrimination is distressing at any age but it can be even more upsetting in adolescence when the young person, who is changing so rapidly, is often more vulnerable to other people's views of their capabilities and their worth. If you suspect that your daughter or son is being taunted, harassed, humiliated or in some way excluded, or if they tell you that this is the case, try to persuade them to talk it through. Make it clear that you are always there to listen and that you do understand. This may be quite painful for you but never brush aside such difficulties in the hope that they will disappear. The young person may be feeling anxious, bewildered, frightened or discouraged and needs your complete support. You will probably find that you have strengths that you can draw on, but you may need support for yourself from family or friends.

In some instances young people feel ashamed that they are the target of such behaviour and need convincing that such incidents reflect badly on others, not on themselves. Do everything you can to build up your son or daughter's confidence and self-esteem, encourage them to be proud of their origins and of themselves and show that you are proud of them too. If you have experienced discrimination yourself you may be able to reassure your child that you do understand just how hurtful it can be but that you have learned to be strong and to come through and so can they. If your own confidence is low because of the difficulties you have encountered, either in this country or your country of origin, it may help to tell yourself just how well you have done in the face of such odds. Developing a more positive view of yourself is one of the best ways in which you can encourage your son or daughter.

It may help to discuss coping strategies with other parents in your community or with your son or daughter's close friends, or with professionals. If problems are occurring in school then you should contact an appropriate member of staff to enlist their help in dealing with the difficulty. If your son or daughter is unwilling for you to do this try to persuade them that it is important for the sake of other young people in a similar position or encourage them to talk to a teacher themselves. If problems are occurring at work encourage the young person to talk to a sympathetic manager or senior person. Whatever the situation, they should not have to cope alone.

Seeking help

You may feel very reluctant to seek outside help if problems are normally discussed only within your own family. However, it may be important to do so if your son or daughter is very distressed or behaving in a way that is quite unlike themselves and you are unable to sort it out. Remember, many young people do experience problems and that you should not feel in any way ashamed of your son or daughter. Although cultural factors may, in some cases, add to a young person's stress, most problems are quite complex and there are likely to be other causes as well. Sharing problems often makes them easier to handle and there may be other parents within your own community to whom you could talk in confidence, or someone with experience in such matters whom you feel you could trust. In some cases professional help may be needed for your son or daughter (see Chapter 9); in other cases the young person may prefer to try approaches, such as healing, for example, which may be accepted within your community.

RUNNING AWAY

Young people run away from home for a wide variety of reasons and often for a mix of reasons. These may include arguments with parents over their lifestyle, worries about exams, fears of bullying, family tensions, sadness over a bereavement, anxieties about their own sexual orientation, problems with money, alcohol or drugs, and sometimes physical, emotional and even sexual abuse. Many young people say they leave home because they feel that no one will listen to what they have to say or because they can see no satisfactory way out of their problems.

If your son or daughter runs away, even for a brief period, it is important not to brush it aside as a youthful prank in your relief at having them back home again. You need to try and understand what made them take that step. Unless they are able to discuss their feelings and anxieties with you or with some outside person and look for other ways of solving their problems, they may well resort to running away again next time they find themselves in a situation which is hard to handle. Try to persuade the young person that you really are prepared to listen, that you will try to be open and flexible, that they have your complete support and that their happiness and well-being come first.

If your daughter or son does go missing you will naturally feel very anxious. Try not to panic. Check first with family and with their friends to see if anyone knows where they might be. Then, if you are still concerned, contact your local police. Depending on the circumstances, the police may search themselves for the young person or may circulate other police stations with details, if appropriate.

If the young person who has run away is under 16 they will be returned to their parents, if they are found by the police, unless there seems a very good reason not to do so. However, young people aged 16 and over cannot be returned home against their will although police will tell their parents if they have been found. If the young person is unwilling to return home the police may provide them with advice and support or refer them to other services. However, many young people only run away for a short time. They often remain in the neighbourhood and return home of their own accord.

Waiting for news of your son or daughter can be extremely stressful, particularly as you are likely to be very worried about their safety. It may help to talk through the situation with someone on the Missing Persons Bureau helpline. They can offer advice and support and also arrange publicity if you wish (see Chapter 15). A number of agencies, including the Missing Persons Bureau, can pass on messages from young people who want to tell their parents they are safe but do not want any direct contact at present.

If your daughter or son returns you may find that you experience very strong feelings of both anger and relief. However, the young person is probably feeling very confused themselves and may find it difficult to cope with such reactions. It will be more helpful if you can remain calm and reassuring. Try to explain that you have been very worried for their safety, that you love them and that you want to understand the reasons that made them leave home so that together you can look for more appropriate ways of dealing with any difficulties.

SCHOOL

Difficulties at home or school can cause considerable stress and unhappiness for young people and may have wider effects than are sometimes realised. For example, they may affect concentration, motivation and relationships and may even give rise to anxiety, depression, school refusal, truanting, disruptive behaviour or other problems. Young people are unlikely to tell teachers if there are difficulties at home; nor are they likely necessarily to confide in parents if there are difficulties at school. It is therefore essential that there should be good communication between parents and teachers so that possible stresses can be identified at an early stage and appropriate help and support can be offered before problems become entrenched.

It is important to encourage your son or daughter and show an interest in their school activities by attending parents' evenings and school events. It will be much easier for the young person to discuss any problems with you if you already have some idea of what goes on at school. Moreover, if you are in touch with their teachers in this way, it will make it easier for you to contact them if you have any worries about your daughter or son's well-being or progress.

It may be that you are concerned in a general way about the young person or that you feel an over-emphasis on good marks or exam results is making your son or daughter highly anxious, for example. Or you may be worried that their under-achievement or a noticeable decline in their schoolwork could be a sign of other problems. If you discover that the young person is causing disruption in class or truanting, for example, it is important to persuade teachers to help you look for the reasons behind their behaviour rather than simply trying to control it. Your son or daughter may need support and understanding because their self-esteem is very low or because such behaviour is their way of showing their anxiety or distress.

In some instances problems can be sorted out by teachers and parents working together with the young person, sometimes with the help of an educational psychologist, education welfare officer or school nurse. In other cases outside help may be needed.

If you are unhappy about the way the school is responding to your son or daughter's difficulties or if the school has threatened to exclude the young person, seek advice from an organisation such as ACE (see Chapter 15). The law is very complex and has undergone many recent changes.

SEPARATION AND DIVORCE

Young people whose parents separate or divorce are likely to feel stressed over a fairly lengthy period. They will probably have been affected by disagreements or tensions leading to the break-up and will certainly take some time to adjust to the changed situation once their parents have parted. Parents may find it difficult to give their children adequate support while they themselves are feeling confused, angry, hurt and vulnerable, but young people do need continued reassurance that both parents still love them and are concerned for their well-being. They may also need convincing that they are in no way responsible for the break up. Some young people do blame themselves quite inappropriately when parents separate, or worry that they should have done more to keep the family together. Try to put some time aside to listen to your son or daughter, however exhausted you are.

Most young people want explanations and information so that they can understand the changing situation and they may feel hurt or resentful if decisions come as a shock. Even if it is difficult to warn young people of an impending separation, for example, parents should certainly make every effort to include their children in discussions directly affecting their future, such as where they are going to live and with whom, how often they will see the other parent and how holidays, family celebrations or pocket money will now be organised.

Many of the changes associated with the break-up are likely to be painful, so parents should try as hard as they can to avoid causing any additional stress or disruption. In most cases young people will have divided loyalties and will feel distressed if one partner denigrates the other or tries to persuade them to take sides. Continued arguments or hostile behaviour in front of the young person, once the separation has taken place, will usually make it even harder for them to adapt to the new situation. You will also need to be very sensitive and tactful about the introduction of a new partner, especially if that person was involved in the break-up. Be prepared to take things very gradually.

Relatives can be an important source of affection, stability and support, so even if you feel angry with your partner's side of the family try to put this on one side and encourage continued contact, where appropriate.

You may be working very hard to make ends meet and are quite likely to feel lonely and depressed at times. Try to get support for yourself, even if it is just talking to good friends, rather than offloading on your son or daughter. They may be very understanding but they will have quite enough of their own emotional stress to cope with.

As far as practical measures are concerned, try to stick to those that are essential. A move to a smaller home may be inevitable but a move to a different neighbourhood may deprive your son or daughter of support from close friends or teachers and needs to be carefully thought through.

If you are not living with your son or daughter it is essential to keep in frequent touch and to assure them that your are there whenever they need you. Continued reassurance that they are still just as important to you – in the form of very regular phone calls, letters or visits – will help them to gradually readjust. Make sure that you do always turn up at the time you say you will so that they know they can rely on you.

However, parents of adolescents also need to be flexible. Young people become increasingly absorbed in their own friends and activities and often shy away from long periods of intense contact with parents, whether they are living with them or not. Short, frequent visits of an hour or so, where possible, may be more comfortable for everyone than whole weekends. You should also be prepared for your son or daughter to change arrangements or let you down at the last moment from time to time. This may be their way of showing their anger because their world has been turned upside down, or it may just be adolescent thoughtlessness. Whatever the reason, do not let communication lapse because you feel irritated or because you imagine that you no longer have anything to contribute. They probably miss you very much and just knowing that you are there for them and that you care is what they most need, whatever their behaviour at any particular time.

Young people may react to the break-up of a relationship in a number of different ways, at different times, and may also experience a number of distressing feelings. For example, they may stay out late, they may form what seem to be unsuitable relationships, they may lose interest in schoolwork or activities or they may seem very tired or depressed. They may feel very lonely, sad or even ashamed about the break-up and they may experience a sense of loss for the family as it once was. In some cases, of course, they may also feel relieved that the tension has now ceased, especially if the relationship had been stressful for a long time. Always inform the young person's teachers and any other professional that they are seeing of a separation or divorce, so that they can offer support.

It is important for young people to have an opportunity to talk about their feelings to an understanding listener. If they bottle them up they may become more anxious or depressed, or may find that they have difficulties in forming relationships in the future. Sympathetic relatives or friends can often offer appropriate support if parents themselves do not feel capable. However, if the young person is very distressed or depressed then outside help such as counselling may be advisable (see Chapter 12).

Although the break-up of your relationship is likely to be distressing for your son or daughter, it is not necessarily responsible for all their problems. Most difficulties have a number of different contributory causes and the break-up may be simply one among many factors. If a young person does have problems it is usually helpful if both parents can discuss how best to handle them and offer support, without recrimination or apportioning blame. You may need to make it clear that you are discussing these difficulties because you are both concerned about your son or daughter, not because you are getting back together, or you may raise false hopes.

SEX AND RELATIONSHIPS

While adolescents will encounter a great deal of pressure from the media and from their peers to prove that they are sexually attractive, parents are likely to worry that they may rush into relationships before they are ready, or that they may take needless risks. Not surprisingly, young people often feel very stressed by the conflicting messages they receive, at a time when they may also be anxious about their changing body shape or confused by increasingly strong sexual feelings.

In addition, young people may experience a number of different anxieties at different times, such as whether they will meet anyone they like and who will like them, whether they are emotionally or sexually adequate, how emotionally or sexually involved they should become in a relationship and what other people will think. They may also worry about the risks of pregnancy and AIDS, and will need information, reassurance and an opportunity to talk things through.

If as a parent you can manage to talk openly about issues surrounding sex and relationships with your son or daughter in a general way from time to time, they are far more likely to come to you for advice and support if a problem occurs. It is quite sensible for you to state your own values in such a discussion, as long as you do so in a calm and reasonable way and as long as you also listen to the young person's views.

Try to encourage your daughter or son to think through what

they want and what is really right for them so that they feel less vulnerable to pressure from their peers and able to say 'no' if they wish. Make it clear that you are always there for them to listen and provide support. You may need to emphasise that they should always come to you first with any problem and that you will always stand by them, however upset you may feel.

Young people often give the impression of being better informed than they really are on matters relating to sex, including the risks of sexually transmitted diseases and facts about contraception and pregnancy. As well as providing information yourself you could give your son or daughter appropriate leaflets or books or leave them around for the young person to read unobserved. They may laugh at your gesture, but they may be secretly grateful for the information.

If your son or daughter is sexually active or likely to become so, you will want to stress the importance of protection both to minimise the risks of conception and to guard against sexually transmitted diseases, whatever your views on their behaviour. Contrary to popular belief, most young people practise sex within a relationship, so you might encourage your son or daughter to visit a clinic such as a Brook Advisory Centre with their partner for contraceptive advice (see Chapter 15).

Although intense, short-lived relationships are common in adolescence, if the young person has numerous brief and not very happy relationships, this may be an indication that something is troubling them that they need to sort out, perhaps through counselling. Brook Advisory Centres also provide counselling for young people with emotional and sexual difficulties (see Chapter 15).

SEXUAL ABUSE

In recent years it has become apparent that sexual abuse of children and young people occurs far more frequently than had hitherto been supposed. It is also clear that its effects are often extremely damaging in both the short and the long term unless understanding and appropriate support are given.

Sexual abuse has been found to be a major contributory factor in many instances of depression, anorexia, anxiety, running away, alcohol and drug misuse, and sexual problems, as well as other difficulties. The young person may be reacting to abuse that occurred at some time in the past, to abuse that has begun more recently or to abuse that has continued over a long period of time.

Sexual abuse occurs when a young person is trapped in a sexual situation where they have no real choice because they are too young, too dependent, too frightened or too confused. The abuser is usually someone known to the young person, often someone within the same family, who would ordinarily be expected to have a protective relationship with the young person concerned and who is therefore betraying a position of trust.

The young person may find it very difficult to seek help because of their conflicting feelings about the person concerned, their anxieties that they may not be believed or that they are some way to blame, and their worries about the distress that such revelations will cause. Abuse by a stranger is comparatively rare and young people will normally report when this occurs. Although it is thought that more girls are abused than boys, it is becoming increasingly obvious that a substantial number of boys are also abused.

Sexual abuse may range from showing a young person pornographic material, or inappropriate touching, or fondling or masturbation, to oral, anal or vaginal intercourse, with or without violence. Generally speaking, the more frequent and the more extreme the behaviour, the more traumatic it is likely to be for the young person, but even incidents that do not involve physical contact, or occur only once or twice, can still be immensely distressing and may have serious long-term consequences. The majority of abuse is carried out by men, but some women do carry out abuse and some young people do abuse others, often as a result of having been abused themselves. It is essential that help should be offered for any type of sexual abuse.

The possibility that their son or daughter has been abused may be so upsetting or seem so improbable and far-fetched to many parents that they dismiss it from their thoughts. But it is very important to keep an open mind if you become aware of disquieting signs and to give the young person every opportunity to talk.

The way a young person reacts to sexual abuse varies from individual to individual and signs of distress are similar to signs that may occur for a number of other quite different reasons. You may notice, for example, that your son or daughter has started to neglect their appearance or that they always seem tired, that they are very withdrawn, that they have difficulties in concentrating, that they cry frequently or seem to have few friends. Some young people become unmanageable at school or at home, while others may overcompensate by striving to be the best in every activity they undertake. Anxiety and depressive episodes are common. The young person might also show their distress through sudden outbursts of anger or aggressive behaviour, through eating problems, promiscuity, self-harm such as slashing parts of their body, running away, recourse to drugs or alcohol, or attempts to take their own life.

Your daughter or son may try to find ways of communicating what is going on by dropping hints, by talking about what is happening to a 'friend' (meaning themselves), or by behaving in an extreme way in the hope of being asked why. They are likely to disclose only a little at first, or to make allegations in a very tentative manner, and may quickly retract if you brush it aside or do not seem to believe what they say. It is vital to be alert to any signs or attempts at communication. You must show that you are prepared to listen and take them very seriously, and that they have your complete support. Many victims of sexual abuse, that went undetected when they were younger, have later declared that what they most needed was to be listened to and believed.

Young people who have been abused often find it a great relief to talk about it to someone who understands, but it is an extremely difficult step for them to take and they are very likely to need a great deal of sensitive encouragement. When you realise what they are trying to tell you, you will no doubt feel very shocked, even if you have half suspected it for some time. It may be tempting to argue with what they are saying, because it seems so unacceptable, but if you do they will clam up, so try for their sake to remain calm and not to express your doubts. Sometimes what they say may seem inconsistent but this often due to stress. Only a very small minority of young people will not be telling the truth. This may be because they were abused when they were younger, without you knowing, and this has confused their reactions, or because they need some other sort of help.

Although the future difficulties may seem insurmountable try to concentrate on the young person's immediate needs. Let them talk about what has happened and describe their own feelings at their own pace, and offer them comfort and reassurance. You may be so upset that you cry with them but try not to let your own emotions overwhelm theirs: they need you to be strong and supportive. You must convince them that you do believe them, that they were right to tell you and that you will put them first, rather than the perpetrator.

Your daughter or son may feel guilty about what occurred, perhaps because they believe that they behaved in a provocative way or because they gained something from the relationship, perhaps even enjoying parts of it, despite their distress. They will need reassuring over and over again that they were in no way responsible for what happened and in no way to blame. Parents who have been abused themselves when younger often find such a situation especially hard to handle because it arouses such painful memories. They need to be sure that they get sufficient support for themselves to enable them to offer their daughter or son appropriate support.

It is important to get help for the young person to enable them to deal with their distress even if the abuse occurred a long time ago, or the alleged perpetrator has left the family home. Quite often symptoms become worse after the young person has talked about what has happened for the first time, but this is usually only temporary if appropriate help is given. If no help is forthcoming problems may continue or resurface in later years. It is also crucial to protect the young person and others from the possibility of further abuse. Such abuse is often addictive and the perpetrator is unlikely to be able to stop without assistance, however much they promise that they will never do it again.

You may have some very difficult decisions to make, particularly if the alleged perpetrator is a close family member, and you are likely to need considerable support. You may find it helpful to telephone the NSPCC helpline to talk to a trained counsellor about the best way forward (see Chapter 15). This may give you enough confidence to approach the GP, social services or the police, who in most places now have specially trained child protection teams, or to encourage your son or daughter to do so.

Once a professional has been informed they are bound to inform other appropriate organisations so that the matter can be investigated. Any necessary steps should then be taken to prevent the abuse from continuing and to help the young person deal with the situation. Very few perpetrators end up in prison, however, as most young people are reluctant to press charges.

In some instances parents may discover that one of their children is abusing another or is abusing a young person outside the family. Such a situation is extremely distressing and difficult to handle but it is vital that the young person who is abusing is offered help by social services or other appropriate agencies in the same way as the young person who has been abused. In fact, it is likely that the young person who is abusing has also been abused themselves at some time in their life. Without help they are unlikely to outgrow this behaviour and it may get worse.

Young people who have been abused are likely to be lacking in confidence and to have low self-esteem. They may be worried that they are in some way different, angry that their childhood has been destroyed and fearful that their brothers and sisters may also be abused. They may be constantly upset by 'flashbacks' which recall the abuse in a frighteningly vivid way. They may feel that their family has betrayed them by not protecting them sufficiently or that they have betrayed their family by bringing matters out into the open. They may be anxious that they may end up in care or that the perpetrator may be sent to prison.

There may also be fears of pregnancy or AIDS, of being unable to relate sexually, of being seen as 'tarnished goods' or of being forced into a particular sexual role for the rest of their lives. Finally they may worry that they in turn may abuse their own children.

Treatment is likely to involve enabling the young person to talk through their problems in a safe setting, as well as the provision of information and appropriate therapies (see Chapter 12). They will need a great deal of reassurance and help to enable them to draw on their own strengths and resources, but with the right sort of support many young people do come through.

As a parent you will also need support to deal with your feelings of shock and pain that your own child has been abused and that you were not able to prevent it. You may feel especially guilty and torn if the abuse was carried out by a person within the family or a person you loved. Try to find someone to whom you can honestly express your own feelings such as your GP or social worker, a counsellor or trusted friend, or telephone a helpline (see Chapter 15). This will make it easier for you to offer support to your son or daughter over this difficult time.

STATE OF THE WORLD

Worries about the environment, wars, starvation, homelessness or the spread of AIDS, for example, may all be indications that your son or daughter is developing into a caring person. Encourage discussion and any responsible activities that aim to raise money or awareness, for example, and enable your son or daughter to feel that they are making a contribution, however small. It is important never to dismiss their concerns, however disillusioned you yourself may feel.

It may be a sign of normal adolescent idealism if the young person seems to be becoming preoccupied with a specific issue to the exclusion of other interests or activities. However, it could also be an indication of some underlying problem, so keep this possibility at the back of your mind. If your daughter or son also seems anxious or depressed, for example, or if they are behaving in an uncharacteristic way and you are unable to sort things out, do not hesitate to seek advice or help, whether from teachers or other professionals, voluntary organisations or other parents or friends.

STEP-FAMILIES

Nowadays, many more young people have to cope with relationships with their parents' new partners and with those partners' own families. These step-relationships, or their equivalent, can be sources of support but they can also contribute to stress. This is particularly the case if the young person has not yet come to terms with the break-up of their parents' relationship, or the death of a parent, or if they have struggled to adapt to living with one parent and feel reluctant to make further changes. Information and advice on handling such matters are available from Stepfamily – The National Stepfamily Association (see Chapter 15).

As a parent you need to give your son or daughter plenty of opportunities to express their concerns, preferably before such changes occur. They may be torn between wanting you to be happy and dreading that their own close relationship with you, or their role in the household, will be taken over by the step-parent. They may worry that this relationship will not last and that you will be hurt again, or they may feel guilty about their other parent if they become too close to a step-parent.

If the step-parent has their own children, who will be included in the family either permanently or at weekends, there are likely to be feelings of rivalry or jealousy as well as irritation at having to take so many other people's needs into account. Young people may well feel confused by differences in attitudes and rules within the step-family and their own household and angry at the prospect of a further move, or indeed of any disruption in their life or invasion of their privacy.

You need to realise that such reactions are quite normal and that it is far better to talk through such feelings openly than to let resentment simmer and spoil relationships. Such matters, and any others that occur, should be discussed in as honest a way as possible with everyone concerned so that you can all find a way of living together that tries to take everyone's needs into account. For example, you may decide that you will set aside a certain amount of time each day, or week, to enjoy doing something with your son or daughter on your own, or that making sure they have their own room is a priority.

You may be worried about the possibility of jealousy or inappropriate attraction occurring between members of the new family. Ideally this should be discussed with your partner before you set up home so that you can both deal with it in a calm and sensible way if it does arise.

If you have come into a family as a step-parent you may feel you are treading on eggshells as far as adolescent children are concerned. It is usually best to take things slowly. Accept that they are likely to resent your presence at times, just as you will probably resent theirs. You can show your concern and that you care by being prepared to listen and give them time. It may be inappropriate for you to discipline the young person but you do need to show you have your own boundaries. Such matters need to be discussed with the adolescent's parent, or parents, where possible.

If a young person has problems that are not directly related to the step-family situation and if you are a fairly recent step-parent, your role may be very much one of offering support. This can enable your partner and the young person, and perhaps the other parent, to deal with the difficulties in the ways that seem best for them. Having someone to lean on who is not quite as closely involved can be a great source of strength and stability.

SUBSTANCE MISUSE
(smoking, alcohol, drugs and solvents)

At some time or other most parents will worry about the risks involved in substance misuse. They are aware that young people today are likely to come under considerable pressure from their peers to smoke, to drink alcohol and probably at some stage, to try out solvents or illegal drugs. They may also realise that such pressures may well be much stronger than when they were growing up themselves.

Your daughter or son is far more likely to respect your opinion if you can show that you are well informed. Relevant information may also help you to put your worries in perspective and enable you to think through carefully any points that you do want to stress. Ask your library or local bookshop about helpful publications, or contact an appropriate organisation (see Chapter 15). If you smoke or drink yourself, for example, it may help if you think why you do so and what it gives you before talking to your children. Unless you are completely honest they are not likely to listen to your views.

Your daughter or son may also be more willing to discuss the problems they face if you can show that you do understand just how difficult it is for any one individual to stand out and be different at the time in their development when being accepted as 'one of the crowd' is so crucial for their confidence.

When talking about such issues to your son or daughter, try to show your concern without seeming to panic or over react. Being over-suspicious, becoming angry or concentrating only on the long-term dangers, for example, may be counter productive and push the young person into more extreme behaviour. Of course this does not mean that you should not talk about the risks or make your own feelings clear. But try and state where you stand in a calm way without seeming to lecture or preach and without closing the door. If you make threats, the situation may well escalate and your son or daughter will feel unable to come to you when they do need your support.

Parents whose religion or culture prohibits substances such as alcohol, for example, may find this kind of situation particularly hard to handle. If they grew up in another country they may well not have experienced the pressures that their son or daughter may face, torn between wanting to observe their own customs and wanting to be accepted by friends. Young people will need their parents' understanding and tolerance to help them through this stage.

It is important to do everything you can to bolster your son or daughter's self-esteem. The more confident they are the more able they will be to resist pressures and make their own choices. Some young people may need to talk through feelings of embarrassment or fears of being excluded if they do not conform or they may simply need to practise ways of saying 'no' in a firm but pleasant way. Others may wish to continue using particular substances but may be prepared to discuss with their parents ways of doing so more safely. Although you may not be very happy with this situation, you will have to accept that only your son or daughter can make the decision to stop. In helping them to reduce the risks you will already have achieved a great deal and you will have kept the channels of communication open.

Young people often start to experiment with substances at the point when they are beginning to break away from their parents and lead their own lives. As a result it is often hard for parents to know just what is going on. Although in many cases the use of certain substances may simply be a passing phase, or one that is well under control, in the case of some adolescents it may indicate more serious difficulties. It is particularly worrying if a young person is using substances on their own, very frequently, and as a escape from some stress of anxiety that they feel unable to face. In such instances they will need help in coping with the underlying problems as soon as possible and before the substance itself becomes a crutch that they are unable to do without.

Smoking

Young people may start to smoke for a variety of different reasons, including curiosity. However, they are far less likely to become confirmed smokers if neither parent smokes. So if you do smoke yourself the best way to help your son or daughter is to give up, if you can. Whether or not an older brother or sister smokes will also greatly influence the young person so it may be worth pointing this out to an older child.

Young people are also less likely to smoke regularly if they know that their parents disapprove, as long as this disapproval is expressed in a calm and rational manner. Nagging or adopting an authoritarian approach may have the reverse effect and push them into smoking.

It is probably not worth concentrating on the long-term ill effects when talking to your son or daughter about smoking; for most young people these just seem too far away. They are likely to be more receptive if you focus discussion on the immediate effects of smoking. These include producing an unpleasant smell that lingers in hair and clothing, making people feel less fit and healthy, and increasing the likelihood of colds and chest infections. You might want to talk about the cost and other ways in which the money might be spent and just how difficult it is to give up once it becomes a habit.

It is important to listen to what your son or daughter thinks they might gain from smoking. If they say it gives them a feeling of confidence then you need to look together for other ways of raising their self-esteem. If they are worried about their weight and have started smoking to control their appetite, you may need to talk about the advantages of a balanced diet and exercise over smoking, as these measures will also enable them to look and feel better.

Sometimes young people smoke to try and deal with feelings of anxiety or with some specific stress. If so, you will want to try and identify any underlying problems with your son or daughter and offer help for these. They may find that a relaxation method is a more effective way of dealing with mild tension.

If you are unable to persuade your son or daughter to stop smoking you may at least be able to support them in trying to cut down. Older teenagers who smoke do quite often want to give up, but may find it very hard if their friends all smoke. You might suggest that they try to limit their smoking to certain social occasions or try to persuade an individual friend to stop smoking with them.

It is important to show your son or daughter that you understand just how difficult it is to stop or cut down and give them every encouragement. You might suggest that they ask the GP for advice on stopping, or ring Quitline (see Chapter 15).

Alcohol

Many parents are not averse to young people drinking alcohol at appropriate times and in moderation. In fact young people often have their first alcoholic drinks at home at some family celebration. Parents do worry, however, if they think their daughter or son may be drinking regularly at too young an age or may be drinking too often or too much.

Because alcohol is such a widely accepted drug, and one which parents themselves may enjoy, young people are often unaware of the real risks involved. It may help if you can find a suitable opportunity to talk about sensible approaches to drink with your son or daughter, as sooner or later most young people will come under some pressure to drink. You are likely to have more influence if you can discuss any issues which may arise in a concerned but calm way without becoming too emotional.

Depending on the circumstances, you may wish to discuss ways of refusing drink, of spacing drinks or of making drinks last, or of asking for non-alcoholic or low-alcohol drinks. Make sure the young person realises that it is advisable to eat before drinking alcohol, as alcohol goes to your head more quickly on an empty stomach and you are more likely to feel sick.

Young people may also feel more in control if they understand about the alcohol content of different drinks. Taking a unit as the measure, one unit equals half a pint of ordinary beer or a pub measure of wine or spirits, for example, though a half-pint of extra-strong beer may equal more than 3 units. They should be aware that the safe recommended weekly limits for men and women are 21 units and 14 units respectively, but that young people who are growing and developing are less able to handle these amounts of alcohol.

Your daughter or son may be more prepared to talk about the risks involved in drinking alcohol if you can do so in a general way without focusing particularly on young people. They do need to know that people are more prone to accidents, even after comparatively small amounts of alcohol, and that it is always safer if anyone driving agrees not to drink at all. They also need to know that people are more likely to have unprotected sex after drinking, and that there is a greater danger of arguments, aggressive behaviour and even violence when people become intoxicated.

They may not be aware that alcohol in large quantities can be lethal and that mixing alcohol with other drugs is very risky as the interaction between two substances is often more powerful than one might expect from the amounts consumed. They also should be warned that if someone becomes unconscious after drinking they should be watched continuously until they can be seen by a doctor. It is crucial to make sure that their breathing is not obstructed, for example by vomit.

Quite often young people will go through a period of experimentation with drink and then settle down. However, a few may begin to drink heavily or become increasingly reliant on drink, and parents need to be aware of possible warning signs. For example, whereas most young people will admit that drinking helps them to feel more confident in a social setting, parents need to think carefully if their son or daughter says they are drinking to unwind or cheer themselves up. They may well be using drink to try and escape from underlying feelings of distress such as depression or anxiety, unaware that alcohol acts as a depressant and will leave them feeling more depressed or anxious and less able to cope than before. It is important to try and persuade your son or daughter to get help for any underlying problems before these are further complicated by excessive drinking.

Most young people drink with friends for social reasons. If your daughter or son is starting to drink alone or in secret, this may well be an indication that drink is becoming a problem. You also need to be alert to this possibility if you find they are drinking during the day or on most days, or if you discover empty cans or bottles in their room which cannot be explained. You may find that they are unwilling to discuss their drinking habits and strongly defend their right to drink as much as they want. Other possible warning signs which could, however, also be signs of quite different problems, include complaints of feeling tired or of headaches or stomach pains, unaccountable mood swings or aggression, loss of interest in work or other activities and inexplicable shortage of money.

Try to persuade your daughter or son to seek help if they do have a drinking problem. Heavy drinking can damage their health even if they are not addicted. Moreover, heavy drinking is also a major factor in many adolescent accidents, mental health problems and suicides. If the young person is unwilling to seek help themselves, look for help yourself on how best to handle the situation (see Chapter 15).

Drugs and solvents

The possibility that a young person is experimenting with illegal drugs or solvents, or coming under pressure to do so, is often a great worry for parents. However, rather than panicking or angrily confronting your son or daughter, your first step should be to ensure that you have accurate information about the substances concerned, especially as these will often be outside your own experience. Knowing the facts will enable you to put your own anxieties in perspective and talk to your son or daughter in an informed way about the effects of a particular substance and the risks involved. There are plenty of helpful leaflets available from appropriate organisations (see Chapter 15).

Research shows that many young people would actually welcome a discussion with their parents on such topics, but careful handling is essential. Even if you feel very strongly about these issues it is important that you do not become too agitated or try to lay down the law as this may result in alienating the young person and pushing them into further experimentation. Your son or daughter is far more likely to listen if you make an effort to understand their point of view and if you stick to facts rather than giving your own opinion. What you are saying about risks will then come over more clearly and it may be that the young person will decide for themselves not to use certain substances, or at least to use them more safely.

It is apparent that many young people, from a wide range of backgrounds, will experiment at some time or other with illegal drugs or solvents and that these will usually be offered to them by friends. However, for the majority this will simply be a passing phase; only a small minority will develop a worrying habit or progress to harder drugs. But parents do need to be aware of the warning signs so that they can step in and offer appropriate support at an early stage.

There is a greater risk that drugs or solvents may become a habit if the young person is using them as an escape from some sort of stress or anxiety. Most young people explore drugs or solvents in a social way with friends to see what they are like and to feel part of the crowd. If you find that your son or daughter is using drugs or solvents on their own or very frequently you need to try and find out whether there is an underlying problem for which they need help rather than simply trying to tackle the use of drugs or solvents.

Of course some young people may resort to more frequent use simply because they are bored. It is important to encourage your son or daughter to find activities that interest them and provide a framework for their spare time, and not to be put off by apparent teenage lethargy. Sometimes spending time alone with them doing a particular activity together can help to spur them on.

In your son or daughter's eyes there may be very little difference between illegal drugs and legal drugs such as tobacco and alcohol, or even the medicines you use at home. But it is important to make it clear that, irrespective of the rightness or wrongness of their views, if they are caught and prosecuted for possessing illegal drugs they will have a police record that could affect their future choices in life.

You may begin to pick up warning signs that all is not well but it may not be clear at first whether these are signs of frequent drug or solvent use or of other adolescent difficulties. If your son or daughter is unwilling to talk about the situation it may help to discuss your worries with your GP or with a helpful organisation (see Chapter 15). Signs may include sudden mood swings or becoming more withdrawn or more excitable than previously, loss of interest in school or other activities, lack of purpose and difficulties in concentrating, loss of appetite, tiredness, looking physically run down, lying and secretiveness. If the young person is buying drugs, you may notice that money or objects are missing from the home or they may try to fund themselves through shoplifting for example.

If you do discover that drug or solvent use has become a habit for your son or daughter try to step back a little and keep calm, however hard that may be. It is important to realise that neither cajoling nor flying into a rage is likely to have much effect. Giving up may be difficult, and only the young person can take the decision to try.

If they do decide to try and give up they will need your full support, as well as professional help, and you should all be prepared for some setbacks. However, if they are unwilling or not ready to give up you may still be able to help them avoid some of the more harmful consequences. For example, you might persuade them to smoke rather than to inject the drug of their choice.

Find out what support and treatment is available for a young person and get support for yourself (see Chapter 15). You will need help to deal with your own feelings of shock, guilt, anxiety and anger and to cope with your son or daughter's behaviour. However upset you feel with the young person for what they are putting the family through, try to keep the doors open. They still need your love and understanding even though this may not be apparent at present.

UNEMPLOYMENT

Young people across the whole ability range now worry about whether or not they will find employment. As a result they may become highly anxious about acquiring qualifications or may on the other hand become less motivated as they see that even qualifications do not necessarily guarantee a job.

Employment brings many advantages that unemployed young people will miss. Apart from obvious benefits in terms of income, employment also gives young people status and a sense that they are now accepted by the grown-up world. Through employment they may have the opportunity for interesting new experiences or satisfying work and they may become more confident about themselves, perhaps discovering unexpected talents or different aspects of their personality. In addition employment also provides a structure to the week and a reason for getting up and going out. Young people who have no job may feel they are simply standing still or even slipping back in terms of confidence and self-esteem.

Parents need to understand that without employment it may be hard for their daughter or son to motivate themselves and to fill their day. They will need a great deal of encouragement and support to try and prevent boredom from setting in and with it feelings of loneliness, futility and the sense that they have little control over their own life. Parents do need to be aware that the longer the young person remains unemployed and unoccupied the more vulnerable they are likely to be to physical illness as well as to anxiety, depression and other problems.

As a parent you will constantly need to build up your son or daughter's confidence and self-esteem. It is important to avoid blaming them for being unemployed or comparing them with friends who have found work. Concentrate instead on doing everything you can to keep them active and motivated by encouraging them to apply for jobs and courses, to take on voluntary work or to pursue sports or other interests as well as contributing to the household chores. Make time to listen, especially if they do seem low, and show that you do understand just how difficult it must be. Get support for yourself if you feel irritated or impatient. It can be very wearing to have an unemployed son or daughter at home, particularly if you are unemployed yourself or working full out to support the family.

PART 3

Mental health problems

If your son or daughter has been distressed or behaving in a way that is very unlike themselves over a considerable period of time, or if they seem acutely distressed for no discernible reason, then there is the possibility that they may be experiencing some form of mental health problem. However, you do not need to wait to be sure before you ask for help. There is often no clear dividing line between ordinary problems and so-called mental health problems but the sooner appropriate help can be offered for any difficulty the better. The longer a problem lasts the more likely it is to become entrenched and the more disruption it is likely to cause in your son or daughter's life.

Signs

Of course, it is not always possible for parents to indentify problems at an early stage, particularly as young people start to distance themselves from parents in adolescence. Even if you do notice odd mood changes, or behaviour that seems rather strange, your son or daughter may resent your concern, deny that anything is wrong or try to conceal their difficulties. You yourself may then be uncertain as to how to interpret such indications. Many signs of distress, when looked at on their own, could also be signs of perfectly normal behaviour. It is usually the combination of a number of different signs, their frequency and intensity that will alert you to the fact that something may be wrong.

It will also become clearer that some form of help is needed if your son or daughter's difficulties start to interfere with their ordinary life. You may find that they are unable to cope with situations at school or work, at home or in their social life, or their behaviour may seem self-destructive, rather than just rebellious, for example. You may also find that ordinary measures such as reassurance from family and friends, talking things through and dealing with obvious problems do not seem to alleviate their distress for more than a very short while.

Another indication that help may be needed is if you yourself are highly tense or anxious for much of the time because of your child's moods or strange or unpredictable behaviour. Most parents can usually distinguish between normal worries about a young person in this age group from worries that things are somehow not quite right. Trust your own judgement and don't be put off by people who think you are being over-protective or fussing. Whatever the cause, you obviously need some support in handling the situation.

Although it is usually a mixture of signs that will warn you of your son or daughter's difficulties, there are also some individual indications of distress that parents should take very seriously. If these occur you should seek immediate advice and help, whether or not you have already noticed other possible symptoms. Such indications include running away from home, which is often a sign that the young person is trying to cope with a problem for which they can see no solution; talk of suicide or attempted suicide (see Chapter 7), or deliberate self-injury, where the young person may lacerate their wrists or forearms for example or damage themselves in some other way; repeated violence to others; eating difficulties (see Chapter 5); and signs such as delusions and hallucinations that may indicate that the young person is out of touch with reality (see Chapter 6).

Labelling

Very often professionals use terms to describe different kinds of behaviour or difficulties. If your son or daughter has been affected by a fairly severe or long-lasting problem you may be relieved to find that it is termed a mental health problem by professionals, or given a specific name, since this may help you to make sense of so much that seemed inexplicable. On the other hand you may prefer to think of your son or daughter as going through a very bad time, as finding it hard to cope at present or as being very distressed. It doesn't really matter as long as your son or daughter receives understanding and appropriate help and support and is seen as a person in their own right with their own qualities, rather than simply in terms of their problems. One advantage of giving a name to a condition is that it can remind both parents and young people that they are not alone in undergoing these experiences, but again it is important to make sure that only the condition is labelled and not the young person themselves.

However, you need to remember that naming a condition may in some cases only serve as a useful pointer. Mental health problems rarely fit into neat categories and it is often not possible to give a clear-cut diagnosis, especially during the adolescent years when so much rapid growth and so many different changes are taking place. Moreover each young person is an individual and each set of circumstances unique. Young people may vary widely in the way they are affected by mental health difficulties and other problems, in their range of symptoms and in the way they respond to treatment or other approaches. In addition, many young people may experience a mixture of problems, sometimes at the same time and sometimes at different times.

Causes

As a parent you will probably be anxious to try and discover the reasons for your son or daughter's problems. But much still remains unknown about the causes of most mental health problems, both in adolescence and at other stages. However, it seems likely that in many cases that there is a mixture of contributory factors, which may vary from person to person. It also seems apparent that in some instances the problem may develop gradually and in others it may be precipitated by a particular stress. Some problems do seem to be a continuation of difficulties experienced in childhood which remained unresolved, while others may take parents by surprise, seeming to arise for the first time in adolescence, perhaps partly as a response to all the demands and changes that are taking place.

Treatment

There are no magic cures for mental health problems and more research is needed to try and identify more effective and appropriate treatments. Professionals, however, can draw upon their knowledge and experience in order to help the young person. They may suggest trying out a number of approaches in order to find those that are most suited to your son or daughter. It is important that you do not pin unrealistic hopes on any particular treatments and expect rapid major improvements to take place. Some treatments may indeed work quickly for some young people, or some young people may simply resolve their problems themselves in the process of growing up, but quite often recovery, when it occurs, is a slow, up-and-down process. However if no changes or improvements take place within a reasonable time or if the young person relapses, you should press for further help.

It will not usually be possible for professionals to predict how long it will take before your son or daughter starts to recover or whether the problem is likely to recur. You may find that this uncertainty is almost unbearable at times, so it is vital to make sure that you have plenty of support. It is also important to remember that regardless of their problems, your son or daughter is growing up and changing, so that if and when they do resolve their problems, you should not expect them to resemble the child they once were. Some young people do emerge from such experiences stronger and more self-reliant; others may need to adjust their way of life and their expectations in order to cope.

Stigma

Mental health problems are far more widespread than is often realised. Most people will know someone who has experienced such a difficulty either within their own family or among their friends or neighbours. Yet, despite this fact, there is all too often a stigma or sense of shame attached to mental health problems which makes it more difficult for both young people and their parents to admit that something is wrong and to ask for help. This is even more the case among young people and parents who come from a background or culture where problems are very rarely discussed outside the family. It is therefore crucial that everyone understands that mental health problems are nothing to be ashamed of and that the sooner appropriate support can be given, the greater the young person's chances of resuming their ordinary life.

The more open you can be about your son or daughter's difficulties – without of course embarrassing the young person or breaking their trust – the more likely you are to discover other parents and young people struggling with similar problems, and the more you will help to overcome the stigma and fear surrounding such difficulties. The pool of support available to young people and their parents might be much greater if parents were able to be more honest and felt less constrained to put up a perfect front.

The next five chapters describe some of the more common mental health problems that may affect young people. They are by no means comprehensive. For example, they do not look at difficulties associated with the condition often referred to as autism by psychiatrists, with problems that may be associated with different forms of learning difficulty, or at problems which express themselves through unmanageable behaviour.

CHAPTER 3

Anxiety

Anxiety is a general term covering a wide range of feelings from mild worry to crippling distress. Because we all expect to feel anxious from time to time we may sometimes underestimate the problems that more severe or long-lasting anxiety can cause, particularly for young people who are coping with so many new feelings and experiences. Anxiety may be the main cause of a young person's difficulties or it may accompany other problems such as depression.

Of course a certain amount of anxiety can be useful in alerting us to take precautions where there is a risk of danger or in helping us to focus our energy in order to tackle new challenges. But too much anxiety inhibits us and sometimes even prevents us from carrying out normal everyday activities.

No one understands all the causes of anxiety and it is not clear why some young people should be more anxious than others. However, in some cases it does seem that a combination of stresses may have contributed to anxiety or that the young person may be especially vulnerable to certain types of stress; while in others the young person's own attitude and lack of confidence may have helped to foster anxious feelings.

There is no precise definition of anxiety but people often recognise they are anxious because they experience a number of physical, emotional or mental symptoms which accompany their anxiety and which often cause additional stress. Each person reacts in their own individual way, but among the many possible physical symptoms that may affect your son or daughter are breathlessness, trembling, dizziness, nausea, stomach churning, diarrhoea, dry mouth, difficulties in swallowing, vomiting, accelerated heart rate, muscle tension and hot flushes and chills. Other symptoms may range from feeling uneasy, irritable, restless and unable to concentrate to worries of not being able to cope, fears that something dreadful is about to happen or even a sense of unreality.

Such symptoms can be worrying and it may reassure your son or daughter to learn that these reactions are quite common. Changes in eating or sleeping patterns or other established habits can also be a sign of anxiety, as can aches and pains and minor ailments for which no cause can be found. If the anxiety is acute or persists for any length of time it can be quite exhausting.

Parents often puzzle as to why their son or daughter should become anxious at this particular stage and the reasons are not always clear. In some cases it may be that the young person was in fact rather fearful as a child, but managed to cope because they were to a great extent looked after and protected. Now, with the increasing expectations that come with adolescence, they find it more difficult to contain their anxieties. In other instances it may be that anxieties start in adolescence as the young person struggles to deal with new and changing situations.

Because anxiety is so hard to measure it is often difficult to judge when it is an ordinary worry which young people can usually cope with by themselves and at what point help may be needed. This is even harder for young people to decide as they are experiencing so much for the first time. Of course a certain amount of anxiety is simply part of life and growing up. If your son or daughter seems a little anxious before a test or a social event, for example, but copes quite well when it takes place and is relaxed afterwards, then there is probably little need for concern. But if their anxiety seems out of all proportion to the situation or seems in some way to be restricting or dominating their life, then help should be offered.

It may be that reassurance from family and friends and commonsense approaches will enable the young person to overcome the anxiety. However, if the anxiety persists, or if it is very distressing, professional help should be sought. The sooner help can be given the better. Anxieties become much more difficult to deal with once they have become entrenched and once young people have developed their own ways of handling them, which may involve adopting certain negative attitudes or compulsive habits and avoiding many situations or activities.

Some reactions to anxiety are described in the following sections. They are only intended as a guide. Each person will react differently and your son or daughter may well not fit neatly into any one category.

CHANGE AND STRESS

If you are aware of some of the situations and stresses likely to cause anxiety for your son or daughter you will be ready to offer understanding and reassurance that may enable them to cope.

New situations

Most people feel anxious in new situations and young people are handling a great many situations for the first time. It may be helpful if you discuss this with the young person in a general way to reassure them that some worry is quite normal. Tackling new situations gradually, one at a time, is usually less stressful than trying to deal with several new challenges at once.

Changes

Major changes caused by a move to a new school or neighbourhood, for example, or upheavals caused by separation, divorce or the illness or death of someone close are bound to cause some anxiety. Parents should show that they recognise the difficulties that the young person may be experiencing and offer reassurance and support. If several major changes occur close together they are likely to be harder for the young person to handle and may cause more severe anxiety.

Stress

Some young people seem to thrive on a range of demanding activities but if they seem at all anxious, you will want to make sure that they are not being pressurised into taking on too much. Try to persuade them that they can say 'no', that it is not necessary to fill every minute and that they do need time for themselves. On the other hand your son or daughter may feel anxious because they are not doing enough. They may feel left out or as though life is passing them by. Encouraging them to take up an enjoyable activity with one of the family or a friend may be a good way of increasing their confidence.

Relationships

Although it is often hard for parents to understand, many adolescents worry about being accepted, not just by close friends, but by a wider circle of peers. Much of their behaviour, which may seem out of character for a while, may be caused by this anxiety. Parents need to be as tolerant as they can and to try to remember that they probably experienced the same worries themselves.

Adolescence is also a time when friendships and relationships often become quite intense although they may also sometimes be fairly short lived. However, this does not make arguments or rejections any the less painful, and difficulties with friendships and relationships do often cause considerable anxiety. If your son or daughter is prepared to confide in you it is important to listen and take them seriously, while at the same time trying to build up their self-esteem. Never brush aside their feelings or tell them they will soon get over this particular upset because they are so young. This will only help to convince them that you do not really understand.

UNDERLYING FEELINGS OF ANXIETY

It is not always possible to relate anxiety to a single cause or even to several causes, especially where young people have anxious feelings for much of the time or frequently become excessively anxious where there is no real need.

You may first become aware that your son or daughter is more than usually anxious because they seem particularly tense or because they develop frequent nervous mannerisms such as pacing, hair twirling or knuckle cracking. Frequent complaints of aches and pains for which no physical cause can be found are another possible sign. You may perhaps find that they are over-concerned about their competence, often in areas where they are perfectly capable of performing well, that they run themselves down and that they demand constant reassurance from others. They may be highly anxious in a general way about the future as well as fearful of specific future events such as tests or social occasions. In addition they may also be unduly pre-occupied with the past, worrying over and over about small mistakes in schoolwork, for example, or whether they said or did the wrong thing.

It is easy to be misled into believing that such young people are mature for their age because they often seem more comfortable in the company of adults. This may simply be because adults seem more reassuring and less threatening than their peers. In addition, the fact that they are often liked and approved of by adults may in part be due to their anxiety to please. They may be much more self-conscious and less confident among their own age group often avoiding participating in class or mixing socially because of their anxieties.

Young people with mild symptoms may manage in most areas

despite excessive worrying. However, if their anxiety becomes more severe it may seriously interfere with school or work and other activities. There is an additional risk that they may become depressed or resort to means such as drugs or alcohol to relieve their anxiety. It is therefore important to seek help at an early stage if possible, before the anxiety becomes entrenched.

There is no single accepted treatment for underlying feelings of anxiety. Professionals are likely to recommend a mixed approach which might include individual, group or family therapy, cognitive behaviour therapy, social skills or assertiveness training (see Chapter 12) and relaxation techniques as well as commonsense strategies such as relieving stress and building up self-esteem.

PANIC ATTACKS

If your son or daughter experiences panic attacks they are likely to feel very frightened, particularly the first time one occurs. A panic attack is a period of intense apprehension, discomfort or fear that often seems to come out of the blue. During an attack, which usually lasts several minutes but can continue for up to an hour, they may suffer from a number of distressing symptoms. These may include difficulties in breathing, palpitations, chest pain, choking sensations, faintness or dizziness, trembling or shaking, tingling or numbness in hands and feet, hot flushes or chills, nausea, feelings of unreality and a fear of going mad or of losing control.

The young person who has had a panic attack may worry that they are suffering from some form of illness. It is sensible, therefore, for them to see their GP in order to exclude this possibility and to discuss ways of dealing with panic attacks. For example, relaxation techniques can usually help to minimise the effects of a panic attack.

Panic attacks can occur in young people who are already showing other signs of anxiety or in those who up till then had not though of themselves as unduly anxious. Because such attacks are unpredictable your son or daughter may worry as much about the possibility of an attack occurring, once they have experienced one or two, as about the attack itself. They may need a great deal of encouragement and reassurance in order to carry on with their normal activities.

Sometimes young people experience some of the symptoms of panic attack because they hyperventilate, that is they breathe in more rapidly and deeply, often due to stress. This lowers the level of carbon dioxide in the body, causing a narrowing of the blood vessels to the brain and reducing the blood flow. They can rectify this by breathing in and out with their hands placed over their mouth and nose. This will increase the amount of carbon dioxide in their blood and regulate their breathing.

WORRIES ABOUT HEALTH AND APPEARANCE

An intense preoccupation with minor physical ailments is one way in which adolescents may show their anxiety. They may worry for example, that a mild headache might be the start of a brain tumour and visits to the doctor may do little to reassure them, or they may genuinely suffer from aches and pains for which no physical cause can be found. In such cases it is important to look for any underlying problems that might be causing your son and daughter to feel anxious, rather than concentrating on the physical symptoms themselves.

Young people may also sometimes express their anxiety through an excessive concern with aspects of their physical appearance. It is quite normal for adolescents to worry about their shape or how they look, particularly in early adolescence when there are so many rapid changes. However, if your son or daughter focuses on a claimed physical abnormality not apparent to others or exaggerates the importance of a very minor blemish and seems to need constant reassurance over a period of time, you should encourage them to discuss with you, or with a professional, other possible underlying causes for their anxiety.

PHOBIAS

A phobia is an acute fear which is quite out of proportion to the object or situation involved. If your daughter or son has a phobia they will be well aware that such a fear is irrational, but will be unable to reason it away. They may suffer extreme anxiety, sometimes accompanied by some of the symptoms of panic attacks, when confronting their particular fear. In addition they may go through agonies of dread simply anticipating the possibility of such an occurrence and worrying about how they would cope. In this way 'fear of fear' further contributes to their anxiety.

The young person may well try to deal with their anxiety by avoiding the feared object or situation. But unless their fear is one which does not impinge on everyday life, this may considerably restrict their activities. Moreover, avoidance often seems to have the effect of increasing the anxiety attached to the object or situation. This in turn may further undermine their confidence.

Why your daughter or son should develop a particular phobia may not be clear. Sometimes a phobia appears after a period of stress or following an illness, but often they seem to occur for no obvious reason. Only in a minority of cases does a phobia seem linked to a specific event or unpleasant experience.

Some phobias, known as simple or specific phobias, involve fear of one thing such as snakes, dogs, air travel, heights or confined spaces. Others, such as agoraphobia, which means fear of public places, may cover a range of anxieties including fear of crowds, of travelling by public transport and of leaving home. Agoraphobia may sometimes start in late adolescence, just as young people are expected to become more independent, and can be quite incapacitating. Social phobia, which involves worries about performing certain ordinary activities in front of other people, can be equally restricting. Young people with social phobia may have anxieties about eating in public in case they choke, worries about writing in front of others in case their hand trembles, or fears about speaking in a group in case they dry up .

It may reassure your daughter or son to know that phobias are in fact quite common. They do sometimes disappear of their own accord after a few months but if they persist for longer or if they are restricting the young person's activities they should seek help. Behaviour therapy techniques can be particularly helpful in treating phobias and in increasing general confidence (see Chapter 12).

SCHOOL REFUSAL

Sometimes young people's anxiety shows itself through a reluctance or refusal to attend school. This occurs across all ability groups and at all ages, although it does become more common in early adolescence. It usually develops gradually. Quite often the young person will have physical symptoms of anxiety such as pains, nausea and vomiting as the time to leave for school approaches. If they remain at home the symptoms will gradually subside and the symptoms will be absent during weekends and holidays.

It is important to recognise that if this occurs your son or daughter is not being deliberately difficult. The young people who have this sort of problem are often those who are well behaved and who work steadily. But they may be lacking in confidence and expect too much from themselves. Perhaps they have found a change of school or a minor setback hard to cope with, or they may be more affected by family stresses such as illness or divorce than you had realised.

You will need to take steps fairly quickly as the longer the situation goes on and the more school they miss the harder it will be for them to return. First check with your son or daughter and the school whether teasing, bullying or other pressures are the cause of their non-attendance (see Chapter 2). If not, discussions with the GP or other appropriate professionals may help your son or daughter identify whether other anxieties or stresses or even depression are causing the problem. Individual counselling, social skills training and family therapy may all be of benefit (see

Chapter 12). Your son or daughter should be supported to return to school as soon as possible, though this may be on a gradual basis if the absence has been a long one.

OBSESSIONS AND COMPULSIONS

If your daughter or son is affected by obsessions or compulsions they probably recognise themselves that their anxieties and fears are exaggerated or senseless. Nevertheless, they will feel quite unable to ignore them.

Obsessions, in the context of mental health, are unwanted and intrusive ideas, thoughts, images or impulses that frequently recur, despite efforts to resist or suppress them. Compulsions are seemingly purposeless behaviours or rituals performed according to certain rules that initially relieve feelings of stress, but eventually cause even more anxiety if the person concerned becomes unable to manage without them. Some young people may have several obsessions or compulsions, or their obsessions and compulsions may change over time. Obsessions and compulsions are frequently associated with depression as well as with anxiety.

It is not clear what causes obsessions but the young person is likely to find them very distressing, particularly as they seem to be beyond their control. Obsessions may take the form of anxieties about contamination, illness or death or harming themselves or someone they care about, for example. Fears of doing wrong or having done wrong and a preoccupation with only having 'good thoughts' and being punished for odd 'bad thoughts' become more common during adolescence.

Obsessions sometimes occur alone but more often they are accompanied by compulsions, or rituals, which are an attempt to alleviate or put right the discomfort and anxiety caused by the obsession. Sometimes there seems to be an obvious connection between the obsession and compulsion, as when fear of contamination leads to the endless scrubbing and disinfecting of objects each time they are touched, while at other times there appears to be no obvious link. Other common rituals are repeated hand washing, touching objects in a specific order and checking and rechecking.

The young person will probably try to resist the compulsion at first or will try to hide it from others. Some young people are able to control compulsions at school, for example, but this takes a great deal of energy and they will probably succumb once they are at home. Rituals can become very time-consuming and may considerably restrict activities and interfere with everyday life and relationships. Quite often the family are drawn into the rituals and participate to avoid upsetting the young person further, but such rituals only relieve anxiety for a short time.

Young people themselves are likely to be very ashamed of their own behaviour if their obsessions or compulsions take hold. It may reassure your son or daughter if you explain that they are not alone and that many other people have experienced similar difficulties. However, this does not mean that you should not take such problems seriously. It is important to persuade your son or daughter to seek professional advice as soon as possible, since such problems are very difficult to deal with without specialised help. Moreover, without such help some young people become hopeless and despairing and may even experience suicidal feelings. Behaviour therapy techniques can be very effective, providing the young person is well motivated (see Chapter 12). If the family have become drawn into the rituals then they should be involved in the treatment.

POST-TRAUMATIC STRESS DISORDER

If your daughter or son has experienced a very distressing event, such as sexual abuse, a violent crime, a serious accident or a human or natural disaster, either as a victim or an eyewitness, they will need help and support to deal with their very painful feelings for some time after the event. It is important to acknowledge the seriousness of what has occurred rather than to avoid mentioning it in the hope that everyone will soon forget.

Make it clear that you are always there to listen whenever they wish to talk, however upsetting this may be. Going over and over what has happened, in a safe and reassuring environment, either with you or with a friend or professional, is one important way to help. You will also want to take every opportunity to build up their confidence and self-esteem.

You need to be aware that your daughter or son may react to a traumatic event in a number of ways. They may have difficulties in sleeping and concentrating; they may become more irritable, watchful and jumpy; they may seem to lose interest in activities they had previously enjoyed or their schoolwork may begin to deteriorate. One consequence of the shock is that they may have repeated intrusive memories or dreams of the incident, or flash-backs in which they feel they are reliving the experience. They may also become acutely distressed by any reminders of the incident, or in some cases may be unable to remember important aspects of what took place. Such reactions may occur soon after the event or be delayed until some time later. It is important to stress that such reactions are perfectly normal, given the circumstances, or they may worry that they are going 'crazy'.

Professional advice or help at an early stage, in the form of individual counselling or cognitive behaviour therapy, for example, may make it easier for the young person to cope and prevent longer-term problems from taking hold (see Chapter 12). Longer-term problems such as the inability to feel strong emotions, a feeling of detachment in relationships and a general sense of pessimism about the future may result if the young person tries to suppress their fears rather than working through them with appropriate support.

WHAT YOU CAN DO

Your daughter or son may experience a sense of relief if you can persuade them to discuss their anxiety. They may have been spending a great deal of energy in bottling up their feelings and in trying to disguise just how anxious they have been feeling in case people laughed at them or thought they were odd. Once it is out in the open it will make it easier for you to offer appropriate support. However, try not to probe too deeply or analyse possible reasons for their anxiety or you may make them more anxious still. You can best help by listening and by reassuring them that they are not alone and that other people experience similar feelings.

Of course, your daughter or son may be very reluctant to talk to you about their anxieties at present. Let them know that you are always available to listen and encourage them to talk to someone else, perhaps outside the family, if it seems appropriate. Meanwhile, take every opportunity you can to build up their confidence.

A young person's anxiety may be partly due to low self-esteem and the feeling that they have no control over their life. This is often the case with young people who are eager to please. They may be particularly anxious as their security depends on the approval of others, rather than on their own self-confidence. It is important to encourage such young people to become more independent and to express their own feelings even if it is less comfortable for everyone else.

There is a very thin line between encouragement and pressure and you need to make sure that you are not adding to the young person's anxieties by focusing too much on whether they pass a certain exam or get a specific job, for example. It is far more important that they gradually learn to deal with their anxieties and cope with a range of situations in a more relaxed way than whether or not they succeed on one particular occasion. If you find that your son or daughter needs more than usual support try to do things with them rather than for them, and step back as soon as you can, otherwise they will lose even more confidence.

Sometimes young people expect too much from themselves or believe that their parents or teachers will only approve of them if they achieve the highest standards. As a result they may feel constantly anxious that they will be unable to maintain their performance or they may drop out because it feels safer to do nothing rather than to fail. Such young people need convincing that it is quite all right to sometimes do less well and to make mistakes. Talking openly about your own failures and mistakes in a relaxed way may be helpful.

Try to praise your son or daughter as often as possible, in a natural manner, and keep criticism to the minimum. If you do have to criticise, always criticise their behaviour rather than the young person themselves and try to do so in a way that leaves them room to change without losing face or feeling that they have somehow failed. Encourage your son or daughter to be proud of aspects of their personality or their activities and show that you are proud of them too.

If you are particularly anxious yourself about certain areas of life you may have transmitted these fears to your son or daughter. Being frank about this and making efforts to tackle your own anxieties alongside the young person can often help.

As well as listening and reassuring there may be some steps you can take that may help relieve or limit some of the young person's anxiety. For example, you might practise situations with them that they find difficult, such as an interview, in the safety of the home or you might help them break down daunting tasks into easy stages which they can tackle at their own pace. It may be that the family have been unwittingly undermining their confidence by making them the butt of jokes and that this will have to change. Or you may be able to help build up their confidence by encouraging them to take up a sport or cook a special meal, for example.

Then there are certain practical approaches that can help to limit or reduce anxiety. For example, you can try to ensure that your son or daughter eats sensibly as lack of food or the wrong food may make them more on edge. It may also help if they cut down or avoid caffeine or alcohol as both can increase feelings of anxiety. Physical exercise will help young people stay fit and reduce tension and some form of relaxation exercise may help them to cope better with stress. You could buy them a relaxation tape or ask your GP to advise. Finally, encouraging them to find an activity that they do well and enjoy is a good way to build up confidence and reduce anxiety.

CHAPTER 4

Depression and Manic Depression

DEPRESSION

The word depression, when used in everyday speech, has a great many shades of meaning ranging from the low mood we all experience from time to time to total black despair. As a result we are often confused as to what other people really mean when they say they are depressed or at what stage we should start to take depression more seriously and ask for help.

It is particularly difficult for parents to judge whether or not their son or daughter is depressed during adolescence as this is a time when the young person is beginning to distance themselves from the family and is therefore less likely to discuss their moods and feelings. Research shows that far more young people consider themselves depressed than their parents realise, and that even when parents know that their son or daughter is depressed, they are often unaware of the depth and intensity of the young person's feelings.

Although there have been many attempts to explain depression by classifying it into different types, perhaps the most helpful way to regard depression in adolescence is as a continuum from normal misery to very severe depression with many stages in between. As a parent you will probably accept that your son or daughter will be down or sad at times; this is simply part of life and growing up. Such feelings may be due to one or a number of causes such as an argument with a friend, failure to be included in an invitation, disappointment over marks in an exam or the aftermath of a recent illness, for example, or may arise for no particular reason that anyone can identify. As long as the young person's reactions do not seem too extreme or last for too long and as long as they appear to be generally taking things in their stride, there is probably no need to worry.

However, if your son or daughter's reactions are more persistent, or if they seem out of all proportion to the actual circumstances, or if their feelings are in some way starting to dominate their lives so that they are unable to cope in any important area such as at school or work, at home or with their social life, you will want find ways to help before matters have the opportunity to become worse. Sometimes just persuading the young person to talk things through with friends and family or with a trusted outsider and offering support and reassurance can be enough to help them come through. But if the depression has already taken a stronger hold then a visit to the GP is advisable as a first step (see Chapter 9).

You may find, of course, that the young person is very reluctant to seek help or even to admit that anything may be wrong. This is a very common reaction among people who are depressed and particularly among adolescents. It may be because they believe that no one can understand how they feel, or because they are ashamed of not coping or because they are convinced that they can manage on their own and perceive offers of help as interference. It is important to explain to them that depression is in fact very common and that many others have experienced similar feelings. You should try to make it clear that depression is nothing to be ashamed of and that seeking help is a perfectly normal and sensible course of action, not a sign of weakness. However, if your son or daughter refuses to see the GP or seek other help, you can ask the GP for advice yourself on how best to manage the situation (see Chapter 9).

Symptoms

It can be hard to tell whether your son or daughter is depressed just from their appearance. Many young people do not in fact look as if they are depressed, despite feeling extremely low. This may be why so many parents remain unaware of just what is wrong, at least in the early stages, unless the young person confides their real feelings.

There are in fact a wide range of symptoms of depression although your son or daughter is likely to experience only some of them. It is the combination of several symptoms, the length of time they have persisted and the extent of their effect on the young person's life that indicates when depressed feelings have progressed beyond ordinary unhappiness and that help is needed. The number of symptoms and the extent of their effect tends to increase as the depression becomes more severe. Young people who are highly anxious or who have other mental health problems may also be depressed or have some of the symptoms of depression.

The onset of depression can be gradual or quite sudden. More girls than boys report symptoms of depression but this may partly be due to the fact that girls tend to be more articulate about their feelings.

Deterioration in your son or daughter's performance at school or work may be one of the first signs of depression that you or others may notice. This may be due to a number of symptoms often associated with depression, such as poor concentration, problems in remembering, decreased confidence, difficulties in making even simple decisions and heightened sensitivity to criticism. You may also find that the young person's sleeping or eating patterns have changed. For example they may complain of being unable to sleep, or sleep in very late, or they may lose their appetite. They may seem permanently tired and lacking in energy, or far more agitated and restless than usual.

Loss of interest and pleasure in ordinary activities, difficulties in performing normal tasks and withdrawal from friends and social contact are common signs of depression. When people are depressed they tend to feel cut off from others as if there were a barrier around them. You may find that your son or daughter tries to spend time alone whenever possible and finds it difficult to express normal affection. Quite often there may be changes in behaviour over a period of time that seem out of character, such as becoming very irritable or withdrawn, overactive or aggressive. Some young people may try to deal with feelings of depression by working too hard, by rushing out each night or even by drinking too much. Aggressive behaviour that may involve breaking rules, lying and stealing can also be part of a depressive episode.

Then there are other common symptoms of depression that you are less likely to be aware of but which will be very distressing for your son or daughter. These may include a sense of emptiness, feelings of failure and worthlessness. They may have very negative views about themselves, believing that they are stupid or unlovable for example, and a sense of hopelessness or very low expectations for the future. They may feel guilty for no apparent reason or may constantly feel regret over some small, imagined incident in the past. They may feel very low and distressed or anxious for much of the time or tense and unwell. There may be recurrent thoughts of death or suicide and, in more severe depression, there may even be specific suicide plans (see Chapter 7).

Some young people may be unaware that they are depressed and express their feelings through physical symptoms such as aches and pains. It is important to be aware of this possibility, but always check with the GP first to make sure there is no obvious physical reason for their complaints.

Causes
You will probably be anxious to try and understand the reasons for your son or daughter's depression but in most cases there are no clear answers at present. We need more research into the roles

that genetic, environmental and temperamental influences might play and into the effects that changes in the body may cause. For example, although we know that there is a great increase in the numbers of adolescents experiencing feelings of depression, compared with younger children who have not yet reached puberty, the reason for this has not yet been established. And although research shows that young people who have a close relative who has experienced depression have an increased risk of experiencing depression themselves, it is not always possible to say whether this is due to genetic or environmental factors.

However, research so far does suggest that while young people may feel down or sad in response to a single event, depression is far more likely to arise from the interaction of a number of different causes that will vary from person to person. It would be quite unusual for a single experience, even one as distressing as the death of someone close, to be the cause of depression on its own. Upsetting experiences do of course contribute to depression but usually in the context of other difficulties or stresses either in the present or the past.

It seems that young people are often more vulnerable to depression if they feel there is no one they can turn to or confide in at times of stress, or if they feel trapped and as if they have no control over events in their life when things are going wrong.

Of course it should not be forgotten that some illnesses or disorders such as diabetes can produce depression or that depression may follow certain illnesses such as influenza or glandular fever, even when the young person has apparently recovered. Drugs prescribed for certain illnesses can also produce feelings of depression as an adverse side-effect. You may also need to remind your son or daughter that alcohol acts as a depressant. If they are drinking heavily to cheer themselves up they may in fact be contributing to their depression.

Treatment

It is important to encourage your daughter or son to seek help as soon as you realise they are depressed. Early treatment can often prevent depression from worsening and alleviate distressing symptoms. Although some depressions may only last a short while if left untreated, others may continue for many months or even several years and there is no way of knowing at the start.

Moreover, not only is depression very upsetting in itself, it is likely to have an adverse effect on various aspects of a young person's development during these formative years. For example, studies or work, and perhaps even more importantly, friendships and social life, are all likely to be affected during a depression. Without help the young person may find it difficult to catch up with work or re-establish their social life, and this in turn may further sap their confidence, making them more vulnerable to depressed feelings in the future.

Unfortunately there has been very little research into the effectiveness of different treatments for young people who are depressed. However, we do know that not all treatments work equally well for everyone, and that this is also true in adolescence. Your daughter or son may respond to one kind of treatment for depression or to a combination of treatments or to different treatments at different stages as well as to supportive approaches at home. You may need to be persistent in order to find what helps. Remember, the vast majority of young people do respond to the right kind of treatment and support. Raising your daughter or son's sense of self-esteem may also help to prevent future depression. However, no one will be able to tell you for certain whether depression will be an isolated incident in your son or daughter's life or is likely to recur.

Your daughter or son will need to talk to someone on their own about their feelings. Research shows that young people are far more likely to give a true picture of their symptoms to a skilled and sympathetic outsider than to their parents, whom they may wish to protect. Encouraging your son or daughter to see the GP if they seem depressed is an obvious first step (see Chapter 9). However, if they are unwilling to do this there may be other sources of help such as a local youth counselling agency (see Chapter 15).

If your son or daughter is only mildly depressed or if the depression seems to be triggered off by a particular worry, then seeing someone such as a GP to talk things over on a regular basis may be enough support. However, if this does not help or if the depression is more deep-seated then some kind of therapy or combination of therapies such as individual counselling or psychotherapy, group therapy, cognitive behaviour therapy, social skills training or an arts therapy may be appropriate (see Chapter 12).

Antidepressants may be offered if a young person has been severely depressed over a long period and the depression has not responded to other forms of treatment, or if they have been very severely depressed for about two weeks or more. Antidepressants are far more likely to be offered to older adolescents (see Chapter 13). Other therapies or support should always be offered alongside antidepressants.

WHAT YOU CAN DO

There is no one right way to handle depression. You will need to find out what works best for the young person concerned but remember they may respond to different approaches at different times. You may find some of the following suggestions useful.

It is helpful if you can find out all you can about depression through reading books or leaflets, for example, and through talking to professionals and to people who have experienced depression themselves. This will make it easier for you to be patient and will enable you to support and reassure your son or daughter, who is likely to be feeling both frightened and bewildered.

It is important that you yourself, the GP, or someone appropriate explains the main features of depression to the young person so that they at least understand that it is the depression that is making them feel or behave in ways that are not like themselves and not that they are really worthless or going 'mad'. Your daughter or son is also likely to find it helpful to talk to people who have been depressed themselves and experienced similar feelings. The fact that such people can say, 'I have been there too and you will come through', can be very encouraging.

A supportive network of family and friends and a close, confiding relationship with a friend or relative can often make it easier for the young person to deal with the depression or prevent the depression from worsening. You may need to explain your son or daughter's depression to family and friends so that they are not put off by the young person's difficult behaviour.

You need to understand that depression will often give people a distorted view of the world that makes it difficult for them to ask for help or accept help when it is offered. They may have all sorts of worries that will seem strange to you; for example they may believe that people close to them are trying to manipulate them. Of course you can't force help on your son or daughter, but don't give up either. You may find that they accept suggestions more readily if they are made by someone outside the family, or you may have to be patient; perhaps they will accept help at a later date.

Try to let your son or daughter know that you recognise that being depressed involves some very painful and unpleasant feelings that no one would choose to experience if they could help it. Show them that you accept that they are not being deliberately lazy or uncooperative. You may need to remind other relatives and friends not to tell them to pull themselves together. As they are not able to do this, such remarks will simply convince them that no one understands. Comparing them with other young people who are coping well at present will also make their situation seem even more intolerable.

You will want to take every opportunity you can to try and raise your son or daughter's self-esteem and convince them that they are loved and valued. This may be by simply being there and offering reassurance and encouragement, by listening if they want to talk and by showing affection if it seems appropriate. The young person is likely to believe they are quite useless and unworthy of being loved and at the same time crave approval and affection. However you should not feel hurt if they seem very unresponsive despite all your efforts. It is probably all they can do to cope with their own feelings.

Accept that this will be a more than usually difficult time for you as a parent as your son or daughter will probably be giving you a double message that is even more pronounced than the double messages that are normal in adolescence. On the one hand the young person may well be saying 'I need your help' and behaving in a demanding and dependent way. On the other hand they may be telling you to 'keep away' and being angry, rejecting and critical. It may seem to you that they are even more self-centred than most adolescents and that they are capable of saying even more hurtful things. However, it is important to remember that this is all part of the depression and that underneath your son or daughter is puzzled and scared. They need your reassurance that things will improve at a time when you may wonder if they ever can.

It may be easier for your son or daughter to talk about how they really feel to someone outside the family who will not be directly affected by what they say. However, if they do indicate that they are willing to talk to you, try to be available to listen there and then rather than brushing it aside or putting it off to another time, however inconvenient it might be. Otherwise you may have lost the opportunity. It is important to listen to what they have to tell you without asking too many 'why?' questions, without interrupting too often and without making judgements. You are quite likely to find that listening to your son or daughter describe their feelings is very painful for you. They may say things that you can hardly bear to hear, but it is important to show that you can cope with what they are telling you for their sake. It will be a relief to them if they can share their feelings. However you may need to seek some support for yourself.

There are certain practical steps that you may be able to encourage your son or daughter to take. For example you may be able to persuade them to take regular exercise in the open air, even if only for short periods. This can help them to remain fit and feel less tense. In addition, exercise often helps to alleviate feelings of depression. You will also want to try to ensure that they eat balanced meals, even if they seem to have lost their appetite, as lack of essential nutrients is likely to make them feel even more depressed. Sleep patterns often become disturbed when someone is depressed. You might suggest that your son or daughter does a relaxation exercise or simply tries to rest if they cannot sleep; worrying about lost sleep will only make them more tense.

Although the young person may feel very lethargic and lacking in energy because of their depression it can be helpful to encourage them to complete a few small tasks each day, even if it is just getting dressed and making a cup of tea, as this can give them a sense of achievement. Although you may be feeling at the end of your tether, try to concentrate on the things they are managing to do, and to praise them for their efforts and any progress.

If the young person is alone for much of the day they will have a great deal of time to brood. It may take their mind off their own problems if they can be where other people are for a time, even if they do not feel able to make much contact. Just going shopping with you, for example, can help to get them out. They may also find that writing down their feelings in a diary each day helps them to make some sense of their experience and gives them a feeling of relief.

The fact that your son or daughter is depressed will be both worrying and draining. It is important to make sure you have your own support and that you don't get pulled down by the depression. Whenever possible you should try to continue to lead your ordinary life and enjoy ordinary pleasures, while still showing your son or daughter the understanding that they need. This will be much more help than if you allow yourself to become gloomy too.

You may well find that you will feel impatient, irritated and even angry on occasion if the depression goes on for a long time. This is a quite normal reaction and you should not feel guilty. However it is important to make sure you have an outlet for these feelings, rather than trying to bottle them up. Talking things over with an understanding friend can often help.

MANIC DEPRESSION

A very small number of young people may experience a condition which is referred to by psychiatrists as manic depression or bipolar disorder. This condition may occur at any time in life from mid-adolescence onwards. It is only very rarely diagnosed in children below the age of 14. Manic depression is characterised by mood swings either to severe depression or to mania, a state of excitement and over-activity, or both, usually with periods of relative normality in between. These mood swings will be much more extreme than those that you might expect your son or daughter to experience in the ordinary way. However, this may be hard to detect in the early stages if the onset is gradual.

It is important to be aware that there is no consistent pattern in manic depression. Some people are affected by extremes of mania and depression, while others find that episodes of depression or mania predominate, or the pattern may alter over the years. Frequency and length of episodes also vary greatly from individual to individual and in the same person over time, making it impossible to predict the future course of the condition in any one person's case. Some people have regular mood swings over a day, a month or a year, for example, while for others mood swings seem quite random, some occurring close together and others with many months or years in between. Some people are affected by a milder form of the condition in which periods of mild mania, known as hypomania, may alternate with periods of depressed mood.

Symptoms

There is a wide range of symptoms in both manic and depressive episodes that vary from person to person and even within the same person during different episodes. Occasionally a young person may experience symptoms of mania and depression at the same time.

Symptoms of depression may include those described earlier in the section on depression, such as loss of energy and motivation, lack of pleasure in activities, reduced concentration, withdrawal from social contact, agitation, changes in sleeping and eating patterns, feelings of guilt and worthlessness and thoughts of death and suicide.

Symptoms of mania may include greatly increased energy and activity, feelings of elation and over exuberance, inflated self-esteem, lack of self-criticism and the normal ability to recognise risks, a short attention span and a decreased need for sleep. A young person may become over-assertive and confrontational or extremely irritable or angry for no apparent reason. You may find that they speak their mind without thinking, even to people they do not know, or are highly critical in a very hurtful way, or even abusive. They may also sometimes become sexually provocative or promiscuous. In the early stages ideas flow rapidly and the young person may seem more than usually amusing and creative. However in later stages thoughts will race and speech will accelerate to become almost incoherent. The young person will be unamenable to reason and behaviour will become increasingly out of control, with a destructive effect on work and relationships. Constant activity and failure to sleep or eat properly can result in exhaustion. In some instances there may be delusions (distorted ideas about the world) or hallucinations (perceptions that others do not share).

Causes

The causes of manic depression are unknown but some research suggests that in certain cases people may inherit a genetic predisposition to the condition which may then be triggered by other factors at some time during their life. However, these factors have not yet been identified. No particular personality type has been associated with the condition.

Treatment

Although there is no cure, early treatment can limit the severity and length of an episode of mania or depression so it is important to encourage your son or daughter to visit their GP at an early stage. Unfortunately it is very difficult to convince anyone experiencing mania that they need help, since in the early stages they will often feel on top of the world and at later stages they will lose insight, so you will need to be very firm. If you explain the situation you may be able to persuade your GP to call.

Manic depression is more difficult to diagnose in adolescence when so many changes are taking place and when young people's temporary reaction to stress may sometimes be quite extreme. Moreover, some of the symptoms, such as delusions and hallucinations, are similar to those which are found where schizophrenia has been diagnosed (see Chapter 6). The GP will probably refer your son or daughter to a psychiatrist for an opinion, or you can ask for them to be referred (see Chapter 9). However, it is likely that even the psychiatrist will want to wait and see if there are further similar episodes before making a firm diagnosis. Hospitalisation may sometimes be necessary if the young person's safety is at risk.

If manic depression is diagnosed it is likely that medication will form part of your son or daughter's treatment. For example antidepressants are likely to be prescribed for severe depression and major tranquillisers for mania. Lithium may be prescribed as a maintenance treatment, if the young person has experienced several episodes of manic depression, to help prevent further episodes from occurring. You or your son or daughter, as appropriate, should be fully consulted about the treatment at every stage and given enough information to make an informed decision (see Chapter 13). Supportive counselling, as the young person improves, will be important to help restore their confidence. In addition professionals should offer support to enable the young person and their family to deal with this very distressing condition. Ask your GP or the psychiatrist who you can all talk to if this kind of support is not offered.

WHAT YOU CAN DO

Because manic depression is fairly unusual in young people you may find that the professionals you first encounter have little experience in dealing with it. This makes it all the more important that you are adequately informed yourself and that you press for specialist help where appropriate. Contact the Manic Depression Fellowship for information. SANELINE or your local MIND group should be able to advise on suitable services (see Chapter 15).

Many of the suggestions already mentioned for coping with depression will apply to the depressed episodes in manic depression. Supporting a young person in a manic episode is likely to be extremely exhausting in a different way because their behaviour will be quite irrational and unpredictable. You may find that your son or daughter suddenly disappears and telephones you some days later from 200 miles away, that they have spent all their savings on bizarre and unnecessary purchases, or that they put on music at full volume at 3 a.m. In addition they may take unacceptable risks and need watching because they are a danger to themselves. Enlist whatever help you can from professionals, family and friends. It is vital that you have some time to yourself to rest and recoup your energy so that you can continue to cope with the strain.

You are likely to feel very distressed, not least because your son or daughter no longer seems to be the person you once knew. It is important to remind yourself that this is part of the condition. However you will need support yourself to help you handle the stress and your own feelings, either from professionals, from good friends who understand, or from other parents who have gone through similar experiences. The Manic Depression Fellowship may be able to put you in touch with a self-help group in your area or you may be able to contact other parents through their newsletter (see Chapter 15).

Your son or daughter is not likely to suffer any physical after-effects from an episode of mania or depression but their studies or work and their social life are likely to have been completely disrupted. Their confidence will probably be extremely low and they will need a great deal of support, affection and reassurance from family and friends in order to get back on their feet.

CHAPTER 5

Anorexia and Bulimia

Because anorexia nervosa and bulimia nervosa are eating problems that involve a great deal of concealment, it is often hard for parents to spot them in the early stages. Unfortunately both conditions can become entrenched, if left unchecked, and both carry considerable risks to health and in some instances to life.

Anorexia, which means 'loss of appetite', is misleadingly named. The person with anorexia eats only a minimal amount, but they remain extremely hungry. In bulimia, which means 'enormous hunger', the person consumes great amounts of food in a very short time. They will then try to counter the effects, often by drastic methods such as self-induced vomiting or the use of large numbers of laxatives. Both problems involve a far more intense preoccupation with body shape and weight and a greater fear of being fat than is normal, even in adolescence. These concerns may take over the young person's life, often to the exclusion of all other interests.

Anorexia most frequently starts in adolescence, although some children as young as 8 or 9 do show symptoms of anorexia, and it can begin in later life. Anorexia is far more common among girls than boys. However, as a parent you do need to be aware that boys can also be affected by anorexia so that you do not miss the warning signs. Bulimia often starts in the early twenties, though it does occur in the teens as well. Again it is far more frequent among girls than boys, but parents should not ignore the possibility of bulimia in boys. You may find that a young person is affected by either anorexia or bulimia, or by a mixture of both at the same time or that they may move on from anorexia, to bulimia, for example. Bulimia on its own is harder to detect than anorexia because there may be no obvious loss of weight.

If your daughter or son is affected by an eating problem you are likely to feel highly anxious, mystified and frustrated. It seems as if the young person, who is often quite rational in other respects, is obstinately following a course of action that results in discomfort and harm to themselves and worry and distress for everyone else, and all for no reason that you can determine. It is important to remember that after the early stages the young person's behaviour is not deliberate. Underneath, your daughter or son is likely to be both frightened and confused. You will need to be very firm, patient and supportive in order to help them deal with the problem.

No one is quite sure how many young people are affected by anorexia and bulimia, particularly as milder cases probably go unreported. Both conditions are much easier to tackle early on so parents should seek help and support as soon as possible. The Eating Disorders Association may be able to advise (see Chapter 15).

ANOREXIA

Quite often anorexia will start with a period of what seems to be normal dieting, perhaps because the young person has put on a little weight or because they want to keep their friends company. Since dieting is so commonplace in our society parents are not usually concerned and indeed in most cases such dieting does little harm since people generally do not stick to a diet for long. However, there are certain young people who discover that they are very good at slimming, for some reason that no one yet understands. Such young people are sometimes unwilling to stop slimming, even when they reach their desired weight. If no one intervenes there is the danger that slimming may take over their life at the expense of everything else and that they will begin to judge their own worth in terms of how far they can control their appetite.

Parents do need to be very conscious of the hazards of dieting, especially during the teenage years, and they should be particularly vigilant if their son or daughter appears to be able to go for long periods without eating and makes excuses to miss their meals. You should try to ensure that your son or daughter eats regular meals and strongly advise them against going on a crash diet. If they must diet try to make sure that they do not lose more than one to two pounds a week and that they stop once the desired weight is reached.

Causes

No one yet understands the causes of anorexia although there is no shortage of theories. It seems likely, however, that anorexia is due to a number of interacting factors that may vary from individual to individual. There is no doubt that pressures to be slim and fit, exerted by the media, are likely to have some influence, at least initially, particularly as the desirable image usually portrayed is of someone below normal weight. It is also suggested that in some cases a fear of growing up and coping with sexuality may contribute to the problem or that young people who have had seemingly happy childhoods may be unwilling to separate from their parents and disturb the status quo, although ironically their anorexia will cause much more disruption than any normal bid for independence. Sometimes changes or upsetting events, or just teasing someone about their weight, may act as a trigger for the anorexia.

Although the personalities of young people who become anorexic do vary, it seems that many of them can be described as compliant, dependent and perfectionist, at least up to the time of the anorexia. Such a young person often seems mature to adults as they are easy, diligent and anxious to please, but closer scrutiny may reveal that their sense of self-worth is almost entirely based on the approval of others. They may see controlling their eating as the one way in which they are able to express their own feelings and control their own lives. It is usually a great shock to parents to discover that the son or daughter they had considered so sensible is capable of behaving in such an irrational and self-destructive way.

Symptoms and behaviour

Fear of fatness: The main psychological symptom of anorexia is a dread of being fat that does not decrease as the person becomes thinner. In fact once weight loss has proceeded beyond a certain point, the young person's perceptions will become so distorted, that even when they become emaciated they will still believe themselves to be too fat. Putting on weight, in their eyes, becomes equated with a dreadful feeling of loss of control, of becoming unlovable or even loathsome. All their energy is focused on becoming 'thin' and controlling their appetite.

Avoidance of food: One of the main ways in which your daughter or son will reduce their weight is by eating very little or eating very low-calorie foods. Quite often they will go to great lengths to disguise from you the fact that they are not eating. For example, they may rush off in the morning before you have time to insist on breakfast, dispose of their packed lunch without touching it, or tell you that they have already eaten at a friend's house. They may try to mislead you by dirtying plates to look as if they have had a meal, and throwing away or concealing the food, or they may restrict their diet largely to fruit, vegetables and salad, for instance, under the pretext of eating more healthily.

One effect that feelings of starvation may have is to increase the young person's interest in food so that they may spend a considerable amount of time studying new recipes and cooking elaborate meals for others. However, they will always seem to have an excuse as to why they do not want to sit down and eat the meal they have so carefully prepared.

Exercise: Very vigorous and excessive exercise is another way in which your daughter or son is likely to try and control their weight. You may be misled at first into thinking that the young person is simply enthusiastic about health and fitness or a particular sport, as is quite normal in adolescence. Warning signs that this may be the start of an eating problem are when such exercising seems compulsive and when it is accompanied by a dwindling interest in food.

It also seems that eating too little can often make people more restless and active. You may notice that your son or daughter suddenly becomes very helpful and thorough in cleaning or running errands, for example, although their schoolwork, which demands concentration, may have started to suffer.

Loss of weight: It may be some time before parents or others notice the marked loss of weight, which is the most obvious symptom of anorexia, as young people are often skilled at disguising this with layers of loose clothing. Even when confronted with their weight loss the young person is likely to make plausible-sounding excuses or deny that anything is wrong.

Other symptoms: One of the signs that may indicate anorexia is that a person's weight is 15 per cent or more below their expected weight providing, of course, that this is not due to an understandable reason such as physical illness. However, it is sometimes hard for parents to judge just what their son or daughter's normal weight should be as this is a time in their life when they are growing and changing so rapidly. Your GP or the school nurse should be able to advise.

One of the most obvious signs for girls that weight has dropped well below normal is that periods, if they have started, will cease.

There is no equivalent sign for boys but they are likely to experience a loss of sexual potency and interest.

Other symptoms, which may increase as weight continues to decrease, may include problems in sleeping, depressed feelings, constipation, headaches, difficulties in swallowing, a slowed pulse rate, lowered blood pressure and greater sensitivity to cold. The young person is likely to appear thin and gaunt, their skin will feel cold, their hands and feet may look blue and they may develop chilblains in winter. A fine downy hair may appear on parts of their body.

Parents may also notice that their son or daughter becomes more irritable or indecisive, or that they become over-concerned with schoolwork or other issues, or that they develop rituals (see Chapter 3). They may withdraw from friends and seem reluctant to leave the home, becoming increasingly emotionally dependent on one or more family members.

Treatment

Early treatment is much more likely to be effective so do not struggle on your own if your son or daughter is continuing to lose weight or failing to put weight back on. Consult your GP. If your daughter or son cannot be persuaded to eat they will need to be referred to a psychiatrist or psychologist with experience in eating problems. Unfortunately there are not many of these so you may need to press quite hard for an appropriate referral.

Your daughter or son will probably look for any excuse to avoid treatment, as they will be frightened that they will be made to put on weight. They may promise to start eating more or to see someone once they have finished studying for exams, for example, or they may assert that if you insist on treatment it means that you do not really love them. It is important to remain very firm and to remember that the young person is not really themself. Anorexia is potentially life-threatening. The longer treatment is delayed, the harder it will be for your child and the longer it is likely to take.

Treatment is likely to involve a programme for weight gain, discussion and support and some kind of therapy. Sometimes the therapy will be started at the same time as the weight-gaining programme, sometimes only after the young person has regained a certain amount of weight although the latter approach is rather controversial. The methods suggested will depend on the circumstances and the views of the professionals concerned. Individual counselling and psychotherapy, family therapy and social skills groups have all proved helpful for anorexia. Some professionals consider that behaviour therapy programmes may be appropriate for some young people. However, research suggests that treatment that involves the family is more likely to be effective (see Chapter 12).

Your daughter or son will be encouraged to eat regular balanced meals, gradually increasing their calorie intake. They are more likely to adjust to a gradual increase in weight until they reach the agreed target. Exercise can be normal but not excessive.

Progress is usually slow and often an up-and-down process. The young person will need regular monitoring, in case they slip back, and treatment may spread over several years. Normally the young person will be living at home, so it is important that parents and other members of the family are involved in the treatment as much as possible, so that they can understand how best to help. Admission to hospital for treatment should be seen as a last resort in case of emergency or when all other avenues have been explored without success.

It will not be possible for professionals to predict how well your son or daughter will respond to treatment. The majority of young people do recover from anorexia in time or improve considerably, though some will retain minor eating problems. However there are unfortunately some people who do not seem to respond to treatment or other forms of support. They remain very underweight or experience episodes of anorexia throughout their lives.

WHAT YOU CAN DO

It is important that you offer your daughter or son your total support and that you do not criticise them for their anorexia. Show them that you understand that they cannot help their behaviour but make it equally clear that you are determined to help them sort out their problems. Being available to talk over difficulties and finding ways to try and raise your daughter or son's confidence can also help.

There may be much that parents can do before the anorexia becomes too entrenched, through adopting a different style of parenting from that which is usually recommended in adolescence. You will need to be very calm and firm and show that you are in control, however anxious and distressed you feel. You may be able to convince your daughter or son that they should eat an agreed amount, particularly if they are fairly conforming. Of course they may then rebel in other areas by becoming rude or uncooperative, but you can deal with this in the normal way, just as you would with any adolescent. This type of method will not necessarily work once the anorexia is well established and you will then need professional advice.

Sometimes young people with anorexia will secretly make themselves vomit after eating a meal. They can become very skilled at vomiting quickly so that no one suspects them. However, once you know that they are doing this you will want to do everything you can to prevent it. One way is to watch them constantly for three hours after they have eaten, but this may not be feasible or acceptable for many parents. Seek advice from an appropriate professional or from the Eating Disorders Association (see Chapter 15).

Remember, secretive behaviour is part of the problem so you need to be extra vigilant yourself. For example, you may need to check your daughter or son's room to make sure that they are not hiding food they say they have eaten. This may well make you feel quite uncomfortable and you will have to remind yourself that it is for the young person's own safety. You should also be wary of any plausible-sounding promises they may make to eat more in the future, rather than eating what is in front of them at the present time. You may feel upset that you are unable to believe them but try to hold on to the fact that their secretiveness and change in personality is due to the anorexia. It doesn't mean that they can never to be trusted again.

Supporting someone with an eating problem does impose an enormous strain. Eating, which should be a source of pleasure, becomes an area of anxiety for parents as well as for the young person concerned. It can often help if other members of the family take responsibility for ensuring that the young person eats certain meals to give parents a break for a while.

You also need to accept that you are bound to have feelings of anger, resentment and even boredom if the anorexia continues for a long time and you should not feel guilty about this. Expressing these feelings to someone who understands, whether a good friend or a professional, rather than bottling them up, can bring a sense of great relief.

Weight loss in anorexia often means that young people can take refuge in more childlike feelings similar to those experienced before puberty and avoid the disquieting emotions associated with growing up. As your daughter or son begins to gain weight these uncomfortable emotions will start to resurface and they are likely to need considerable support and understanding in order to cope with them successfully, especially if they are facing them at a later stage than most of their contemporaries.

Because your role in persuading your child to resume sensible eating habits can be so crucial, it is easy to let their eating difficulty take over your life. You can begin to feel as obsessed by food as your son or daughter because of the responsibility. Moreover, the young person may have become very manipulative because of the problem and draw you into their way of responding to situations in a way that may be unhelpful for you both.

It is therefore very important to have support for yourself so that you can step back a little and lead your own life. Talking to

other parents who have had similar experiences can be very helpful. There may be a support group near you run by a hospital, for
example, or the Eating Disorders Association may be able to put
you in touch with such a group (see Chapter 15).

BULIMIA

Bulimia appears to be closely related to anorexia as a problem. In
fact as already mentioned, some young people experience both
problems at different stages of their life or are affected by a mixture of symptoms of anorexia and bulimia at the same time.
Although the person with bulimia is obsessed by the fear of being
fat, those affected by bulimia on its own usually manage to keep
their weight within normal limits.

The causes of bulimia are not yet understood, but there are
likely to be a number of contributory factors, which may vary
from person to person, rather than a single cause. It is often hard
to detect bulimia. The person concerned may go to great lengths
to hide their behaviour, which they recognise as unacceptable
although they feel powerless to change.

If your son or daughter is affected by bulimia they will experience periods of compulsive 'binge' eating in which they will
consume large amounts of food in a short space of time. The
food selected is often the most fattening and the sort of food that
they would usually deny themselves. This compulsive eating goes
far beyond the bounds of normal greediness with the young person devouring several loaves with lashings of butter and jam,
packets of biscuits, tins of fruit, cakes and boxes of chocolates,
for example, either ignoring or unaware of signals from their
body that they are sated. Such episodes are usually planned ahead
and carried out in secret when they are sure that they will not be
disturbed.

The young person is likely to feel very guilty and ashamed at
their loss of control and may try to counter the effects of over eating by self-induced vomiting, which sometimes brings them a

sense of relief. They may also take heavy doses of laxatives or diuretics under the mistaken impression that this will help to rid the body of excess calories. Vigorous exercise and a period of strict dieting often follow a binge.

Sudden extreme swings in weight caused by bingeing and dieting are bad enough for health but the methods used in bulimia to try to reduce weight are particularly risky. Vomiting, laxatives and diuretics all serve to rid the body of water, disturbing the balance of fluid in the body in the process and causing the loss of essential mineral elements. Overuse of laxatives can cause persistent tummy-ache and damage to bowel muscles. Persistent vomiting will dissolve tooth enamel and can damage muscles and kidneys.

Your son or daughter will probably feel very ashamed of their chaotic eating habits but be unable to remedy them without help. Concentration is likely to be affected and school, work and relationships may all suffer because of the secrecy involved. Your son or daughter may well feel very depressed, and suicidal thoughts are not uncommon, so it is important to try and persuade them to seek help as soon as you recognise the problem.

Many of the points made in the previous sections on 'Treatment' and 'What you can do' for anorexia will apply for bulimia too. Treatment will involve encouraging the young person to establish a regular eating pattern and to maintain a steady weight without starving or bingeing and vomiting. A mix of approaches may be more effective. These might include individual counselling, group therapy, cognitive behaviour therapy or behaviour therapy, for example (see Chapter 12). Treatment is likely to be on an outpatient basis and the family should be involved. It is important to be aware that some young people who appear to be dealing with their bulimia then go on to alcohol abuse. Parents need to be vigilant if the bulimia appears to be receding but the young person is drinking more alcohol and seek advice.

CHAPTER 6

Out of Touch
with Reality

As a parent you are likely to feel both alarmed and at a loss if your daughter or son shows signs that they are becoming 'out of touch with reality', as you perceive it. Such indications may include garbled or incomprehensible speech, bizarre or increasingly withdrawn behaviour or the reporting of confused or strange thoughts or ideas.

Try to stay calm as any agitation may upset the young person further and worsen the situation. There are a number of reasons why your son or daughter may be reacting in this way and you need to be alert to the various possibilities so that you can offer appropriate help without seeming to criticise or panic.

Possible reasons

It is more common than is generally realised for young people to behave in odd or uncharacteristic ways that may seem quite 'crazy' for a few days or so, perhaps due to some sort of stress or anxiety or inability to handle their feelings. However, because it is often difficult to communicate with young people at this age, it can be hard for parents to judge whether this is likely to be a brief, passing episode associated with growing up or warning signs of more serious difficulties. If the young person seems to return to their former self very quickly, then there may be no need for great concern. Of course, parents should try and find out what may be worrying the young person and offer support. They also need to keep a watchful eye for any signs occurring in the future and to seek help if they do.

Misuse of alcohol, drugs or other substances can cause young people to behave in strange ways. You will want to find out if this is a possible reason for your son or daughter's behaviour (see Chapter 2).

The young person's behaviour may be due to an episode of mania, although psychiatrists will usually want to wait and see if there are further similar episodes before making this diagnosis (see Chapter 4). Distorted ideas about the world or perceptions that others do not share can also occur in episodes of very severe depression.

Sometimes young people may experience an episode of being 'out of touch with reality' which may last for several months and which turns out to be their way of reacting to some sort of stress, or to difficulties in growing up and establishing their identity, or to some trauma in the past such as sexual abuse that they have never disclosed to you. It is important to seek professional advice as soon as possible and it will help if you can think of any reasons why your son or daughter may be so distressed (see Chapter 9). If the problem can be identified and help offered and if the young person can learn more appropriate ways of dealing with future problems and expressing their feelings, then the chances of making a good recovery are high.

It may not be possible for psychiatrists to tell you at an early stage whether they consider your son or daughter's symptoms are mainly due to a reaction to some kind of stress or to other reasons or whether they are likely to be experiencing what is referred to as an episode of schizophrenia. However, if your son or daughter has previously been coping well and has been active and popular and if acute symptoms seem to come from out of the blue, there is a good chance that they may not reappear.

Schizophrenia

This is the name given by psychiatrists to a distressing condition or group of conditions in which the different parts of the mind no longer seem to function together in the way most people take for granted but become confused and disordered. As a result the person who is affected may begin to distrust their own sensations and reactions or the behaviour of those around them. They will become bewildered and frightened and often increasingly uncertain of the difference between what is going on in their own imagination and what is occurring in the outside world. Most psychiatrists will not make a diagnosis of schizophrenia in young people unless they have observed several episodes over a period of time.

You will probably hear the term 'schizophrenia' frequently misused in everyday speech to describe people with split or multiple personalities who switch rapidly from one complete and convincing personality type to another. Such an occurrence is rare and has nothing to do with the psychiatric term 'schizophrenia', which implies that the person's original personality may well become less recognisable for a time as thoughts, impulses, memories and emotions become increasingly jumbled and disjointed.

You should not be surprised to find that there is a great deal of controversy about the nature of schizophrenia, both among psychiatrists themselves and among mental health organisations and pressure groups, due to the fact that so much still remains unknown about this very distressing condition for which no very satisfactory treatment has yet been discovered.

Researchers are not yet agreed as to whether they should regard schizophrenia as a single condition or as a group of closely related conditions, and the causes of schizophrenia have not yet been identified, although many suggestions have been made. Inheritance may play some part in contributing to schizophrenia, at least in some instances, although just how this occurs is not yet clear. Research does show that children of a parent who has been diagnosed as having schizophrenia do have an increased risk of developing schizophrenia, whether or not they are brought up by that parent. It is also possible that stress may act as a contributory factor as a highly stressful event sometimes precedes the first episode of schizophrenia, although in other instances there may be no obvious form of stress.

The view that certain types of family upbringing could result in schizophrenia has caused parents a great deal of guilt and distress in the past but is now far less widely held by professionals, due to lack of any clear evidence. However, it is generally accepted that families do have an important role to play in providing a calm and supportive environment, once the condition has been identified, as people diagnosed with schizophrenia tend to be highly susceptible to any form of stress and to react adversely to conflict, pressure or sudden change.

Conditions diagnosed as schizophrenia can start at any time in life but the first episode most commonly occurs during the later teens or in young adulthood. Although equal numbers of men and women are affected, men seem to develop schizophrenia at an earlier age. The onset of schizophrenia may be sudden or it may develop over time, with the person gradually appearing less able to concentrate, more withdrawn and less able to cope.

If the psychiatrist suggests the possibility of schizophrenia or makes a diagnosis you will obviously be very anxious to know what the future may hold for your son or daughter. However, it is not possible to predict the course of schizophrenia. Some young people will recover completely and experience no recurrence of these problems. Others will manage well with only occasional relapses or with a reasonable amount of support, but may not lead quite as full a life as they might otherwise have done, while a minority, unfortunately, will be more seriously affected and need a considerable amount of support throughout their life.

Symptoms

There is a wide range of symptoms associated with schizophrenia or with young people being 'out of touch with reality' for other reasons. These symptoms may vary from person to person and often in the same person at different times. Many of the symptoms on their own may have no particular significance. It is the combination of various symptoms, or their severity or the length of time that they have persisted that will indicate to you that your son or daughter needs help. Other symptoms may alert you because they are more unusual or extreme. However, there could be different explanations as to why your son or daughter may be experiencing a number of symptoms so psychiatrists are generally cautious about making a diagnosis until they have had time to look at various possibilities and have seen how the condition develops.

Among the puzzling symptoms that you may notice is odd or disconnected conversation that is hard for others to follow or make sense of. This may arise because the young person discovers they are unable to think clearly because their mind is bombarded with so many different ideas or because it suddenly seems to go blank for no apparent reason. You may also find that the young person is preoccupied with some philosophic problem to the exclusion of other interests or that they seem to be investing trivial or chance events with particular significance.

Your son or daughter may find it hard to concentrate for long and it may become apparent that their studies or work and their relationships are beginning to suffer. For example, they may rush frantically from one activity to another without completing anything, or they may withdraw from social contact, seeming to lack energy and motivation and spending long periods of time on their own doing very little or just staying in bed. You may notice a lack of concern with their appearance and personal hygiene or you may find that they sometimes seem to grimace or make odd movements or that they have become obsessed with what they regard as an imperfection in a part of their body that seems quite normal to everyone else or with a very minor blemish.

You may become concerned because the young person seems to be expressing their feelings in a way that seems odd or uncharacteristic. For example they may seem overexcited and exuberant, or have odd outbursts of anger for no apparent reason, or become aggressive or very occasionally violent, or you may find that they have become withdrawn and self absorbed. In some cases it may seem to you as though the young person's feelings have become rather blunted so that they are never particularly happy or sad or it may be that you are surprised by your son or daughter's inappropriate reaction to a situation, either failing to respond at all or laughing at a sad event and crying at a joke.

Your son or daughter may experience disturbances in perception, sometimes referred to as 'hallucinations', when they hear, see, smell, feel or taste things that are not apparent to others but which are quite real to them. For example, they may hear voices commenting on what they are thinking or urging them to take certain steps. These voices, which may be friendly or hostile, may seem to come from within their own head or from somewhere outside. The young person may carry on silent conversations with the voices or converse with them out loud.

Sometimes young people develop distorted ideas about what is actually happening which may be described as 'delusions'. For example, they may become convinced that outside influences are controlling their thoughts, inserting ideas into their mind, or broadcasting what they are thinking to those around them. Or they may believe that everyone is whispering about them wherever they go, that they are being pursued by secret agents or that someone is plotting to harm them. You may find that no amount of reassurance or rational argument changes their view.

However, before assuming that every bizarre idea is a delusion or hallucination the psychiatrist will need to look at other possible reasons why the distressed young person may seem to hold such a belief. Some very strange ideas may simply be due to lack of knowledge or misunderstanding of certain facts or the young person may have a very vivid imagination and simply decide to be uncooperative. In some cases a belief which seems improbable at first may in fact be a valid response to an actual situation. Young people who are being bullied or racially harassed, for example, may well express feelings of persecution. And finally it is important for any professional to check whether the young person is expressing ideas and feelings in a way that may be perfectly acceptable within their own culture, however strange they may seem to those from a different background.

Treatment

Try to persuade your son or daughter to see the GP as soon as you realise that something may be wrong. Although young people who are 'out of touch with reality' may not think that they need help, or are too anxious or frightened to seek it, there may be times when you are able to communicate and get their agreement, even when they are at their most distressed. Make sure you accompany them to the GP to offer support and to press for an appropriate referral to professionals who have experience in dealing with such difficulties (see Chapter 9). If they are unwilling to see the GP, go yourself to discuss how best to handle the situation.

Early advice and help is essential to ensure that young people who are changing and developing so rapidly spend the least possible time with a distorted view of the world. It is far easier to resume normal activities and friendships after a short break than a long one. In addition, in the case of what is termed schizophrenia, there is some evidence that the length of an episode can be curtailed by early treatment.

Regular discussions or counselling should be an important part of your son or daughter's treatment right from the start, whatever the cause of the young person's problems. This should be with an appropriate professional who can provide your son or daughter with explanations and support and who can help them to establish some sort of structure in their life as they begin to get better. You should ask for this type of help if it is not offered. The young person may also be encouraged to catch up with missed education or to participate in a range of activities in order to regain confidence. Social skills training and arts therapies may be particularly helpful (see Chapter 12).

Treatment should also involve work with the young person's family. Professionals should offer information, advice and support and discuss ways of helping to ensure a calm, supportive atmosphere that will assist recovery. Where schizophrenia is suspected or diagnosed by the psychiatrist, it is even more important that the family is helped to find ways of avoiding tension, as far as the young person is concerned, as any conflict can exacerbate the condition. Families may also need help in dealing with feelings of anger or sadness about the situation or in coping with uncertainty about the outcome.

If your son or daughter is experiencing acute, or 'florid', symptoms, as they are sometimes termed, such as delusions or hallucinations, and schizophrenia is suspected or has been diagnosed by the psychiatrist, they are likely to be offered medication. Antipsychotic drugs can help to control these symptoms but they should be used with the greatest caution, especially with young people. Parents, and the young person where possible, need to discuss the situation carefully with the psychiatrist concerned and weigh up the benefits of such drugs in curtailing a condition that may be damaging, against their adverse effects (see Chapter 13). Medication is also likely to be offered if manic depression or very severe depression is suspected or diagnosed (see Chapter 4).

Medication, however, has no effect on certain symptoms that may also be associated with schizophrenia, such as apathy, lack of motivation and lack of concentration. There is a considerable risk that such symptoms may become entrenched if the young person is affected over a fairly long period, and they will then be much harder to deal with. Providing the young person with just the right amount of stimulation and structure to their day, without too much pressure, may go some way towards preventing this.

Your son or daughter is most likely to continue living at home while they receive treatment. However, they may be admitted to hospital for a short period in order for professionals to try and make a diagnosis, or they may be admitted if they become very distressed or seem to be a danger to themselves or others. Most young people will be admitted as informal patients; very occasionally they may be detained (see Chapter 11).

Your son or daughter may come from a very different culture from the professionals they are seeing. If so, it is essential that you, or someone from your community, accompanies them to the initial interviews to explain the young person's background. Otherwise there is a risk that your son or daughter's ways of thinking and expressing emotion, which you take for granted, may be misunderstood. As a result, they may be given inappropriate treatment, perhaps being prescribed drugs unnecessarily or even being admitted to hospital, or important symptoms may be missed.

WHAT YOU CAN DO

It is important to press for appropriate services and the right kind of support if your son or daughter is behaving in strange or unpredictable ways. Services are sparse and you may have to be very persistent, but it is crucial that your son or daughter receives the right kind of help and that you yourself have some support. Contact Young Minds, SANELINE, or your local MIND group for advice (see Chapter 15).

It is important that you have the opportunity to talk on a regular basis to a member of the professional team who is seeing your son or daughter so that you can better understand what they are experiencing and how best to offer help. You also need to know what you should do in a crisis. Many professionals welcome the opportunity of working closely with parents and other family members, without of course breaking confidentiality (see Chapter 9). However if you do experience difficulties either in finding someone who is prepared to talk to you or in getting the information and support you need, write to your son or daughter's consultant psychiatrist or contact SANELINE, your local community health council or MIND group for advice (see Chapter 15). Don't be put off. After all, you have the main responsibility for caring for your son or daughter and you have the right to advice and support.

It will help if the whole family has as much information as is available from an early stage and can openly discuss the best ways of handling any difficulties. It is likely to be more worrying for family members if you try to pretend everything is normal than if you honestly share your concerns and what information you have. Remember that brothers and sisters are likely to need support. It can be helpful if they can talk to someone outside the family about their own feelings.

Expressing anger, irritation or even very natural feelings of anxiety in the young person's presence will usually make the situation worse. People in a very distressed state can barely deal with their own emotions, let alone respond to those of other people, however reasonable they may seem. Each family member therefore needs to find a means of expressing their own feelings away from the young person, rather than bottling them up. This might perhaps be through confiding in a friend, through writing in a diary or through digging in the garden, for example. They may also need to learn to step back a little and pursue their own interests, at least for a time, to give the young person space, while remaining calm and supportive.

Parents are often so anxious and upset that they sometimes forget that the young person is feeling very frightened and distressed themselves and is not being deliberately difficult. You will need to be very tolerant and supportive. However, this does not mean that you should collude with any strange behaviour or ideas. Indeed, to do so may confuse the young person further. If you find certain behaviour upsetting or unacceptable you can tell them so calmly while making it clear that you are not criticising

132

them as a person. In addition, if your son or daughter describes 'voices', for example, you can say gently, but firmly that you understand that they are hearing them but that you cannot hear them yourself. It is important that you do not let yourself be drawn into their way of viewing the world as you may then begin to wonder what is real for you. Moreover, this will not help the young person. What your son or daughter needs, above all else, is people around them who have a firm contact with reality.

All parents will find it hard to cope with the uncertainty over the future course of the condition, particularly if schizophrenia has been diagnosed. It may help if you can somehow develop a way of living from day to day. You will need to reduce your expectations of the young person so that they do not feel a failure, while still gently encouraging them to undertake a number of activities to keep them stimulated. If it seems that they are unlikely to recover completely then original plans for studies or work will need to be modified to avoid undue pressure. This can be very hard for all parents to come to terms with, but it is often particularly difficult for parents where the young person seemed especially talented. It is quite normal to feel painfully disappointed in these circumstances but try to conceal this from your son or daughter. They will have enough disappointment of their own to deal with.

It is important to show your son or daughter that you understand that they are battling with difficulties and that trying to cope with hallucinations or delusions, for example, can be both frightening and exhausting. Remember to praise them for small achievements or steps forward and try not to become too disheartened over lapses.

However, it may sometimes appear as if all your support and patience make no difference to your son or daughter who perhaps no longer seems able to show any affection or express any interest in what is going on. Try to hold on to the fact that they do need your support although they may not need your presence all the time. They are simply so bound up with their own problems that they have no energy left for others. It is important that you pursue your own life and interests as far as possible; if you can detach yourself a little you will feel less drained and more able to offer support when the need arises.

As your son or daughter starts to recover they will need help to establish a routine that has enough variety and stimulation but is not too taxing. Where possible this should include some form of exercise, since this will help them to feel fit and good about themselves. Their confidence will be very low so you will want to look for ways of helping to build up their self-esteem and encouraging them to become gradually more independent.

It is a tremendous responsibility to care for a son or daughter who is very distressed and whose behaviour is odd and unpredictable. You may find that you are highly anxious for much of the time, at least at first, and that you sometimes feel guilty or depressed. At times the strain may seem almost unbearable and coping with crises can leave you feeling shaky for some considerable time (see Chapter 8). Moreover, if it seems that the young person is unlikely to recover completely you will of course find it very painful to try and come to terms with all the changes that this may entail. It is important, therefore, that you take all the help and support you can get; you will need to unburden yourself frequently either to good friends or to a professional. If your son or daughter seems likely to be affected in the long term, then joining an appropriate support group, such as an NSF group where you can meet other parents, may be a help (see Chapter 15).

CHAPTER 7

Suicidal Feelings

There may be a fear at the back of your mind that your son or daughter has suicidal thoughts or even actively contemplates suicide, particularly if you are aware that they are under stress or having difficulties in coping with a mental health problem. Perhaps you find it difficult to voice such worries because they are so frightening, or because you believe other people will think you are over-reacting, or because suicide itself is such a taboo subject. As a result you may feel even more anxious and alone.

However, a surprising number of parents have probably experienced similar anxieties and recognise all too well those feelings of panic or dread when the young person fails to appear at the expected time or doesn't respond to calls. Such anxiety is likely to be even more pervasive if the young person has already made a suicide attempt or has talked about suicide. Any mention of suicide, even in a joking way, should always be taken seriously.

It is important that as a parent you do have someone in whom you can confide these fears, who won't simply brush them aside. Such a person might be a good friend whom you can trust, a professional or someone from a voluntary organisation with experience in this field such as the Samaritans (see Chapter 15). If you can confront your fears and talk them through it may help you to offer more appropriate support to your son or daughter should the need arise. Such support will almost certainly include encouraging your son or daughter to talk and listening to them without offering advice or making judgements, even though what they are saying may cause you a great deal of distress.

Listening

Young people are often reluctant to disclose their deeper feelings, especially to parents, but you should make it clear that you are always there to listen if they wish to talk about anything that may be worrying them. However, before they will open up your son or daughter needs to feel confident that you will really give your full attention to what they have to say and that you will take their feelings seriously. It is also important that you avoid the temptation of arguing with them that things cannot be as bad as they make out or of trying to reassure them that they will feel better in the morning. This will only convince the young person that you cannot understand what they are going through and may leave them feeling even more isolated and alone.

Of course, it is very painful as a parent to hear your daughter or son describe their desperation or distress. But it can be a great relief to the young person to express their real feelings, perhaps for the first time, and to find that you are strong enough to listen and offer them support. You should try not to interrupt unnecessarily, but simple questions such as, 'What are you feeling?', 'How long have you felt like that?' and, 'What would you like to be different?' may encourage them to continue talking. If you are concerned about the possibility of suicide you can ask if they have ever thought of harming themselves. If it has been on their mind they may find it a tremendous relief to talk about it; if they have never seriously considered it, your question will not make it any more likely.

Such a conversation will be very worrying for you but it is even more worrying if you do not know what is going on in your son or daughter's head. You will be bound to feel distressed but try to share your feelings with the young person so that they realise that you are upset because they are upset, not because they have disturbed your life. Putting your arm round your son or daughter, or hugging them, if appropriate, can often help.

If they do admit that they have thought of taking their life, try to get them to explain why. Rather than arguing about their reasons, which may make you both even more upset, tell them that you accept that this is how they see things, but that it is not how you view them. Emphasise over and over again how much they mean to you and how much you love them and ask what you can do together about the situation. If they are not already seeing someone try to persuade them to get some outside support.

ATTEMPTED SUICIDE

If your daughter or son does make a suicide attempt you are likely to feel very shaken, frightened and perhaps even angry. But the young person will need your understanding and support more than ever. Don't be fobbed off by suggestions from others that it was just attention-seeking behaviour, or even a mistake. It is right that you take what has happened very seriously and do your best to find out from the young person just why they felt so desperate. Let your daughter or son know that you are there to listen and to try and understand, and that it will be much easier for you all to put it behind you once you have talked it through.

The young person may not always be clear why they have made a suicide attempt and there may have been no obvious warning signs. Often the trigger may be quite trivial, such as a minor argument over rules, or a tiff with a friend, but the real causes are likely to be more complex with a number of contributory factors that may include past experiences and present stresses.

There are some young people who may try to take their own life because either recently, or over a period of time, they have felt that they wanted to die. This is quite often because they have been very depressed and because the future seems to them to be quite hopeless. Others may attempt suicide because it seems to them the only way out of an intolerable situation, although they would not choose to die if they could see another alternative. Then there are those young people filled with despair who see it as the only way of communicating the pain they feel. Young people experiencing strong emotions or difficulties for the first time are quite often overwhelmed. Moreover, they lack the experience to handle problems and the confidence to know that they will come through. They may also be more likely to act on impulse than an older person. Some few may see a suicide attempt as a way of changing a situation and other people's feelings towards them.

It is not known how many suicide attempts there are since not all incidents will be reported. However, about 90 per cent of attempts that are reported consist of drug overdoses. If your daughter or son has taken an overdose and there is the slightest risk go straight to your hospital's casualty department. Some drugs such as paracetamol can cause serious damage even though the young person is quite conscious.

Although young people with difficulties such as severe depression, heavy drinking, substance abuse, eating problems, and conditions which may be diagnosed by psychiatrists as manic depression or schizophrenia, may be more likely to try and take their own life, many young people who do make suicide attempts are not affected by such conditions. However, this does not mean that they do not need help. If your daughter or son has been in hospital after a suicide attempt, they should be seen by a member of the psychiatric team before they are discharged, to discuss the situation and further possible help. If this does not happen ask for an appointment to talk things over, or ask your GP what steps you can take. The GP may refer the young person for an assessment or may suggest some counselling or other appropriate support.

It is crucial that the young person should not be left high and dry to cope with the same situation on their own that led to the suicide attempt in the first place. They will certainly need your support and they may well need some professional help. The telephone number of a person or an organisation, such as the Samaritans, that they can contact if they feel desperate and you are not available is an additional safeguard (see Chapter 15). It is estimated that about one in ten young people will make a second attempt within the next two years, and of these a small minority will succeed. The risk of a young person making a further attempt can be lessened if appropriate help can be offered, although you may need to be extra vigilant for a while about your son or daughter's moods and behaviour and take care to remove obvious risks such as certain drugs from easy reach.

As a parent you should accept that you may need some support for yourself in dealing with your own very mixed feelings about what has occurred, perhaps from a member of the team who is seeing your son or daughter, or from your own GP or a voluntary organisation. It may help to talk through how you can allow your son or daughter the space and independence they need, while at the same time containing your own anxiety about their safety.

SUICIDE

Finding that a young person has taken their own life comes as an overwhelming shock to parents and other family members and to others who were close. Even those who only knew the young person slightly are likely to feel immensely distressed. Everyone will be left asking why and trying to make sense of what seems such a senseless action and such a terrible waste.

Looking back, many parents can identify warning signs that all was not well, though it may not have been clear to them at the time just how despairing their daughter or son really was. In a few instances, however, the suicide may seem to come 'out of the blue', causing even greater bewilderment because the young person had appeared to all those around them to be happy and coping well and had given no indication of inner distress.

It is impossible to make generalisations about young people who take their own lives. They come from every kind of background: from close, caring families as well as from more deprived circumstances, and include those who are able and popular as well as those who have always experienced difficulties in coping and making friends. It seems likely, however, that at the time many such young people do feel worthless, for whatever reason, and believe that the world would be better off without them, perhaps quite unable to take account of the feelings of loss and devastation that their death will cause. Some idealistic young people may also simply feel too overcome with despair at the world situation to want to go on living.

Sometimes parents may have been aware of the risk of suicide but have been powerless to prevent it. The young person may have talked of suicide or they may have made a previous attempt, but this time they were more determined. Or they may have been grappling with longer-term problems such as eating disorders, heavy drinking or drug abuse, or conditions diagnosed by psychiatrists such as schizophrenia, depression or manic depression. Parents may have taken what precautions they could but no one can keep watch 24-hours a day over a period of time. Sometimes they may understandably have relaxed their guard as the young person seemed to be coming out of a depression. However, this, unfortunately, can be a dangerous time as the young person now has the energy to carry out the act that they lacked when they were very depressed.

There are no accurate figures to indicate how many young people take their own lives since the Coroner will only record a verdict of suicide if it is absolutely clear that the young person intended to take their own life. Otherwise a verdict such as 'accidental death' or an 'open verdict' will be recorded (see Chapter 14). The younger the person the less likely it is that a verdict of suicide will be given. It seems that girls are more likely to end their lives through drug overdose, whereas boys are more likely to use more violent means. More girls than boys attempt suicide but more boys are recorded as ending their lives through suicide.

Those who are left

If your son or daughter takes their own life you will almost certainly be left with a great sense of emptiness and isolation, and experience a number of feelings over a period of time that may be very hard to bear. There may be numbness and disbelief at first, followed by intense pain and grief. You may feel that you are going round and round in circles asking questions for which there are no answers, such as, 'What made them do it?', 'What actually happened?' and, 'Why my child?', until you begin to doubt your own sanity.

You may blame yourself because your daughter or son is no longer there to blame, and feel guilty because you were unable to prevent what occurred. Since most parents see their role as one of nurturing and protecting their children, you may even feel you have failed as a parent and believe that others think so too. The world may suddenly seem a very unsafe place and you may have a feeling of doom, as though you were waiting for the next tragedy to occur, or you may feel that you do not care very much whether you live or die.

When parents are in this sort of state it is very hard for them to meet anyone else's emotional needs, and the emotional needs of other children are often completely overlooked, although parents may become very anxious about their safety. Yet these children will also be grief-stricken and will need a great deal of support and encouragement to talk through their feelings and to try to come to terms with their loss.

It may help if parents can ask a relative or good friend whether they can give extra support to brothers and sisters in this situation and they should also make sure that their children's school, college or workplace are aware of what has occurred and can offer sympathetic understanding. Counselling, even if only for a few sessions, can often be a great help. Ask your GP what is available. If young people are allowed to bottle up their feelings or to try and pretend nothing has happened they are likely to experience considerable problems at a later stage.

There is also the added risk that a brother or sister who is extremely distressed may try to emulate the young person who has taken their life with the idea of being reunited with them. It is vital to keep tablets or any weapons safely locked away.

Family members may find it difficult to communicate because they will each be so involved in trying to handle their own grief. Some people need to keep busy, others to talk compulsively and others to cry alone. However, they should at least try to explain to each other that they need to grieve in their own particular way. Otherwise resentment and misunderstanding can sometimes arise, with some members believing that others are not really upset at all. They also need to be aware that in searching for reasons it is all too easy to blame other members of the family, either directly or indirectly, for contributing to the tragedy, just at the time when they most need each other's understanding and support.

Friends and neighbours can help by listening and showing affection and by doing practical tasks such as shopping. As in all crises, you may find that some people are a tower of strength and can always make time to listen. However others, who you might have expected to offer support, hurtfully avoid you or avoid acknowledging what has happened. This may be due to embarrassment, but the result may be to make you feel that you are in some way an outcast. People need to be aware that a card or letter just saying they are thinking of you can be a great comfort and that just being with you and sharing your grief, and perhaps later your happy memories, will mean a great deal. It is also helpful if friends can remember to contact you or to send a card on the anniversary of your daughter's or son's death.

When you feel ready to do so you may need help to talk about your innermost feelings. Some parents have found that counselling has given them the support they need. Others have found that talking to other parents whose children have also taken their own lives has been the greatest help. Just realising that these parents, who are ordinary, normal people, have shared the same devastating experience has helped them to start to feel normal again themselves and to begin to hope that they too will come through. The organisation known as Compassionate Friends may be able to put you in touch with a group of such parents in your area or a parent you can talk to over the telephone (see Chapter 15).

Grieving is an up-and-down process. Just when you think things are improving you may re-experience the anguish as clearly as on the day it happened. Expect the anniversary of your daughter's or son's death, their birthday and other family celebrations to be difficult times. Accept that you are bound to feel 'if only' when you hear that one of their friends is getting married or expecting a baby, however unselfish you may want to be. Many parents who have gone through this experience say that it took them between 18 months and two years before they felt that they were even beginning to live again, although perhaps with a very different set of values and in a very different way.

PART 4

How parents can cope

CHAPTER 8

Stresses for Parents

You will almost certainly feel very anxious yourself if your son or daughter is affected by a mental health problem, or some other serious difficulty. It is important to accept that this is a worrying time for you and that you may experience a great deal of stress. In addition to your worry over the young person, you will probably feel that you are being pulled in different directions by conflicting demands. You may be struggling to be available to support your son or daughter, while desperately trying to give enough attention to your partner or other children, for example, or continuing to fulfil commitments at work or elsewhere. It is important to get whatever help you can so that you are not shouldering all the responsibility for your son or daughter. Remember that you need to look after yourself as well. If you become too low or exhausted you will be unable to manage.

Involving the family

Try to involve your family and others who are close so that they understand what is going on and can offer you and the young person appropriate support. The more open you can be as a family in discussing the problem, without in any way blaming your son or daughter, and the more information you all have about the particular difficulties, the easier you are likely to find it to cope.

It is vital to remember that brothers and sisters are likely to be very upset by the young person's problems, even if they appear to show little interest. If you feel too stressed or anxious yourself, try to ensure that a relative or understanding friend is available to listen, if they wish to talk, and to offer appropriate support.

Your son or daughter's distress may absorb almost all your energy and it may often feel as though it has taken over your entire life. This in turn may cause a great deal of strain between you and your partner, if you have one, just at the time when you need each other's support the most. It may help if you can step back a little from your son or daughter and try and put aside some time for your relationship with your partner, however difficult that may seem. You might be able to persuade a relative to take responsibility for the young person, to enable you to have some evenings on your own together, or even a few days break. If you can relax and give each other some much-needed attention, this will probably benefit your son or daughter too, in the long run.

If you are on your own, as a lone parent, you are often at even greater risk of becoming completely overwhelmed by the young person's difficulties. Make sure that you make time for yourself in order to recharge your batteries and get as much support for yourself as you can.

Each member of the family will have a different relationship with your son or daughter and may be able to offer help in their own particular way. However, sometimes there are quite fundamental differences within a family about whether or not a young person has a problem, why they are behaving in a particular way or whether they need any outside help. You are likely to feel very lonely or hurt if your partner, or other members of the family, are unwilling to recognise your son or daughter's difficulties or if they blame you for the way you brought them up or for how you are trying to handle the situation. If this is the case get some support for yourself. You are likely to need help in trying to decide what is best for your son or daughter. Sometimes a good friend or a professional can see the situation more clearly and may be able to persuade members of the family to co-operate more closely in order to help your son or daughter.

Distressing feelings

You are bound to feel very vulnerable if your daughter or son develops a mental health problem or some other serious difficulty. Your own role as a parent, your relationship with the young person and their future may suddenly all seem far less certain, and this on top of all the other changes taking place during adolescence. For some parents it may seem as if their world has been turned upside down. You will need a great deal of reassurance and support during this time.

Guilt: In addition you may be upset to discover just how guilty you feel about your son or daughter's distress or how much you blame yourself for their problems. You may find yourself going over and over their earlier years, searching for clues that perhaps things were not quite right even then or worrying about individual episodes that you might have managed differently. This may be because you feel so responsible for your son or daughter or because you are desperate to find any explanation for their problems. It is quite common for parents to blame themselves at first and you may simply have to work through these feelings. After a time you may be able to accept that the causes of most problems are very complex, that you cannot shield your children from every difficulty, and that as a parent you probably did the best you could.

Nevertheless, you should talk to an understanding friend or get some help for yourself if you find you are continually going round in circles. Dwelling too long on negative aspects of the past will sap your confidence and leave you with less energy to cope. You may need encouragement to look instead at all your positive achievements as a parent and all the strengths you can draw on in order to help your son or daughter at the present time.

Worry: If your son or daughter has been distressed for a long time or if their problems tend to come and go you may find that there is always a worry at the back of your mind. During calmer periods it may seem as if your anxiety is under control but it will usually rapidly increase if there is even a hint that things may be going wrong, sometimes becoming an almost constant preoccupation. Although you are likely to remain anxious for as long as your son or daughter experiences such difficulties, you will find it easier to cope if you can stand back a little from their problems and remember that your own needs are important too. Try to get as much practical and emotional support for the young person as you can. Your worry will be much greater if you are their sole support.

Reactions to tactless comments: You may well find that you are quite often distressed by tactless comments or well-meaning but quite inappropriate advice from people who know little about mental health or even about adolescents. Such people are often looking for simple explanations or for someone or something to blame. Sometimes they may pick a reason, almost at random, it seems, for your son or daughter's difficulties, such as that you pushed them too hard, or not hard enough, or that you went out to work when they were younger, or that you stayed at home and gave them too much attention. Sometimes they may even dispute the fact that the young person has any problems because they look so normal, or tell you that they have nothing to be distressed about. Try if you can to find a way of halting such conversations rather than becoming involved. They are an added irritation and upset that you can well do without.

Loss of spontaneity: At times you may find that you are trying so hard to avoid upsetting your son or daughter, or to organise situations so that they are more manageable for all concerned, that you lose your own feelings of spontaneity. It may even seem to you that you have no right to enjoy yourself while your son or daughter is troubled. But you will have far more strength to draw on if you are able to make some time for yourself to be a little lighter or to do what you want to do.

Loneliness: You may feel very isolated as you struggle to cope with a difficult and changing situation. It may sometimes seem to you as if yours is the only family undergoing such an experience. Affection and support from friends or relatives may be crucial. If that is not available, for any reason, make sure you do get support for yourself either from professionals or from appropriate voluntary organisations (see Chapter 15). If you can make contact with other parents in similar circumstances you may find that you are able to offer each other a great deal of mutual support.

Grief: You are likely to feel very distressed yourself if your daughter or son is very unhappy or behaving in a strange or self-destructive way, and you may often ask yourself why this should happen to your child. There may be particularly upsetting times when you feel quite powerless to help, although you would do anything you could to make things better.

You may also experience an acute sense of loss because your son or daughter no longer seems to resemble the young person you once knew, or because they show no signs of fulfilling their earlier potential, even allowing for all the changes that take place in adolescence. You may also find it extremely painful when, for whatever reason, you are forced to compare your son or daughter with other young people of the same age who seem, at least on the surface, to be leading happy, normal lives. Accept that these feelings are natural and have a good cry, if it helps, or talk to an understanding friend. You can't be strong and coping all the time.

Anger: If your son or daughter's problems continue for some time you are likely to experience a number of rather uncomfortable emotions that may include irritation, resentment, boredom, anger, feeling trapped or even wanting to walk away. It is important to recognise that these are quite normal reactions to a very demanding situation and you should not feel guilty. In fact, if you expect only to have positive feelings towards your son or daughter you are bound to feel inadequate. Find some means of expressing your feelings away from the young person rather than bottling them up. Such reactions do not mean that you no longer care about the young person; rather, that at times you find their behaviour extremely difficult or exasperating.

Delayed reaction: You may be rather bewildered to find that you feel unaccountably anxious or down as the young person starts to recover. Perhaps the least little thing may bring you close to tears or to snapping someone's head off. One reason may be that you drew on all your reserves of strength in order to cope and are now feeling quite empty and exhausted. Another possibility is that, as things begin to improve, many of your own anxieties, which you held in check during the stressful time, may now begin to emerge. You will need understanding and support from those close to you to help you adjust to the new situation and deal with your own needs.

Relationship with the young person

It is important to remember that mental health problems and other serious difficulties can be very frightening for young people. Your son or daughter may sometimes feel as though their feelings, moods or behaviour are outside their own control. Moreover, they may also be convinced that they are the only young person who has ever undergone such an experience. You may be able to reassure them that, although they are unique, others have encountered similar problems and have come through.

It helps if you can remain very calm and encouraging, however worried you may feel. Showing your own anxiety is likely to upset the young person further. They are also likely to become more distressed if you criticise them for anything related to their condition or if you give vent to emotions such as irritation or anger in their presence. Your son or daughter will find it difficult enough to struggle with their own feelings. They are unlikely to be able to cope with other people's reactions.

Each young person will react to their problems and to the circumstances in which they find themselves in a different way and you will have to find your own method of offering support. It will help to listen to suggestions from professionals or other parents, for example, but in the end you will have to use your own judgement. You will probably discover what works best through trial and error, and you may also find that different approaches are effective at different times.

Relationship difficulties: You may find that your daughter or son turns on you in a hurtful way in order to express their feelings simply because you are the person closest to them and the one with whom they feel most safe. They may continually criticise what you are trying to do, for example, harangue you over incidents that took place a long time ago or heatedly accuse you of faults, some of which may be imaginary and some real. Try to avoid either colluding with the young person or being drawn in to lengthy arguments in which you try to justify yourself or are made to feel guilty. However, it is important to be able to accept that you may sometimes do things in relation to your son or daughter that turn out not to have been for the best. In such cases you need to be able to say firmly to the young person, or even just to yourself, 'I did what I thought was right at the time', or, 'I was at the end of my tether and not acting very sensibly, but that can happen to anyone', rather than endlessly blaming yourself.

If there have been difficulties in your relationship with your son or daughter over a period of time, then some outside help may be needed specifically to help you sort this out. If, however, the tensions seem to be of recent origin, then now may not be the best time for deep self-questioning or searching self-criticism. You will need all your energy to support your son or daughter. However, outside help will still be useful in suggesting new approaches that may improve the situation and enable you to cope. It may be helpful to look more closely at what is going on in your relationship with the young person at some later time, when you are a little less stressed.

You need to be aware that your son or daughter may make it very difficult for you to help. They may behave in ways that often seem even more self-centred and manipulative than many ordinary adolescents or they may be so withdrawn or confrontational that it is hard to get through. Sometimes they may give you the impression they are co-operating and you may feel very let down when you find that this is not the case. However difficult or unrewarding it may seem, it is important to remember that your son or daughter is very vulnerable and does need your support.

Style of parenting: You may find that it is appropriate to develop a very different style of parenting from that usually recommended in adolescence. For example, you may need to remain far more involved with your son or daughter than you had anticipated at this particular stage in order to bolster their confidence or to help provide them with a more supportive structure to their day. The young person's sense of self-esteem is likely to be very low and they will need constant reassurance, even if it seems to you to have little effect. You may find that they respond best if you are very firm and lay down boundaries for behaviour that is under their control, while remaining totally accepting of their problems. Remember, your son or daughter is likely to feel a failure when they compare themselves with brothers or sisters or with friends. They need recognition and encouragement for the fact that they are struggling with difficulties. You will want to praise any small improvements.

It is important to avoid identifying with your son or daughter's problems or being drawn into their world. You will be much more help to the young person if you can detach yourself a little and keep your feet firmly on the ground. It will help if you can spread the responsibility for supporting your son or daughter, and make time for at least some interests of your own.

Independence: Young people with mental health problems or other serious difficulties are unlikely to be able to cope with all the different ways in which adolescents are expected to show greater independence. They may be reluctant or unable to take on greater responsibility for themselves, and parents will often find that they need to be more vigilant because of their son or daughter's vulnerability. Don't listen to people who tell you you are being too protective. Your son or daughter needs your support and is likely to need help over matters such as making appointments and getting to places on time. However, it is important to avoid the temptation to take over completely, either because the young person wants you to or because it is easier to cope that way. Except when your son or daughter is extremely low or distressed, you will want to try and encourage independence and responsibility at least in small everyday matters, otherwise they may lose what little confidence they have. You need to find a way of doing just enough to enable them to do whatever they can for themselves, however long it takes. Of course you will want to minimise obvious stress but where they do need help try to do things with them rather than for them wherever possible. You will need to back off gradually as they start to recover.

Progress: If problems have lasted for any length of time it may help if you try and live in the present as much as you can and avoid setting goals for the young person for the future. Progress may well be slow and uneven, or occur in quite unexpected areas, and if your expectations are too high, or too rigid, you are bound to feel disappointed. On the other hand, if you can take each day as it comes you may find that you are able to respond more realistically to the young person's actual needs. You may also find that you are more able to enjoy the here and now at times or take pleasure in small things with your son or daughter.

It is often difficult for parents to relinquish the aims they had for their son or daughter, but it is far more important for the young person to achieve some sort of happiness and stability in their lives than to acquire certain qualifications, for example. However if recovery is very slow or seems likely to be incomplete you will probably need considerable support to adjust and come to terms with the situation.

You will also need to be very patient. Even when a young person seems to have greatly improved, they may still have to catch up on the experiences they have missed out on while they were struggling with their own problems. As a parent you may find for a time that you are dealing with feelings and behaviour more suited to an earlier age.

Crises

Depending on your daughter or son's problem, there may be extremely difficult times when they are very severely distressed, or perhaps even a danger to themselves or others. Each situation will of course differ but it will help if you know who you can call on for support, whether it is a good friend, the GP or a professional the young person is seeing, or someone on a crisis helpline, for example (see Chapter 15).

You may find to your surprise that you are able to act in a fairly calm and almost detached way because you know you have to cope. Even so, be prepared to feel very shaky and drained once the worst is over, you are then quite likely to experience the emotions that you suppressed in order to manage and may well feel more anxious than you did at the time. Sometimes fears or frightening images may pop up unexpectedly during the day or overwhelm you at night. It may help to let yourself go and have a good cry, beat a pillow or go over and over what occurred with an understanding friend. If crises are fairly frequent you will have the added stress of worrying when they may recur and what form they may take. It is important to realise that you may continue to need a good deal of support between crises and not just at crisis time.

You may find it helpful to write down exactly what occurred

soon afterwards, while your memory is still fresh. This may help you explain the situation more clearly to relatives or professionals. In addition it is easy to wonder later if you over reacted or did the best thing, particularly if your son or daughter is angry at any decision you made on their behalf, such as taking them to hospital. With a record you will probably be able to say, at least to yourself, that you did what you felt was for the best, under very great stress and in a situation where there seemed to be little real choice, and that is the most any parent can be expected to do.

Looking after yourself

Although you will want to offer your son or daughter as much understanding and support as you can, you must make sure that you look after yourself too; otherwise you are likely to end up both physically and emotionally exhausted.

It is vital that you safeguard your own health. Try to eat regular, balanced meals and if you find your sleep is disturbed, make sure that you do at least rest. Practising a relaxation technique may help to calm you down. Regular exercise will keep you fit and give you more energy to cope. Exercise is also a good way of relieving tension and helping you to sleep.

Everyone has to find their own way of dealing with stress. Some people prefer to keep quite busy doing practical things while others may need long walks by themselves or in the company of friends. You will have to work out your own priorities but you should not feel guilty if you spend less time cleaning or preparing meals, for example. Let those close to you know how they can best help, whether it is by spending time with your son or daughter or by taking over some of the chores. However, you should be prepared for the fact that your own feelings and reactions may be rather unpredictable. There are likely to be some days when you manage less well, whatever steps you take.

Your own feelings of confidence may be quite low if your son or daughter is very distressed, and worrying all day will probably make things worse. Doing your own work or pursuing your own interests can be a way of taking your mind off the young person's problems for a while and restoring your own feelings of self-esteem. You need to know that you have value as a person in many different ways and not simply just as a parent. You may also find that you can support your son or daughter better if you can step back a little and try and lead your own life. If you are with them all the time you may find that you are increasing each other's feelings of tension or anxiety.

Life can sometimes seem very grey and you can feel weighed down by responsibility if your son or daughter's problems continue for a considerable time. Try to find ways of recharging your batteries by doing something for yourself that you really enjoy or that enables you to feel calm. This might be as simple as having a leisurely bath, staying in bed a little later than usual, buying yourself a small bunch of flowers or making time to listen to some favourite music. These are all ways of confirming to yourself that you matter too and can often help you to feel a little more positive.

Support for yourself

You will need a great deal of support for yourself in order to cope with the worries and uncertainties about your son or daughter. Such support may come from close friends, professionals or from a voluntary organisation or a helpline for example (see Chapter 15). It is important that you have someone you can trust who will listen to you in confidence and be with you at whatever stage you have reached. You will probably find it a great relief to talk to someone who will acknowledge the difficulties you are experiencing and who will accept that you feel the way you do, without passing judgement on either you or your son or daughter. You may continue to need such support from time to time, even when the young person starts to recover, as you still may feel quite anxious and lacking in confidence.

It can also be reassuring to talk to other parents, perhaps in a support group, if one exists, or through personal contact. Just knowing that other parents have had similar experiences and understand just what you are going through can be a great comfort and make you feel less anxious and alone.

Coming to terms

There may come a time when you feel the need to try and make some sense of your experience and look at whether there is anything you may have learned, despite all the distress you have undergone. You will probably be aware that you have changed your priorities in life and that what matters to you now is rather different from what mattered in the past. You may find that you are able to live more fully in the present and that you can draw on strengths that had previously been untapped. Finally you may also discover that you have a fund of common sense and wisdom to offer others, having been forced to try and cope.

PART 5

Help, information and services

I t is often difficult as a parent to know where best to turn for information and support when your son or daughter is distressed or behaving in a strange or worrying way. The following chapters outline the type of help available from both professionals and from voluntary organisations and briefly explain the main treatments offered and some relevant legal issues.

Of course, you may also find that help is forthcoming from a variety of other sources including friends and family, other parents and people from your community. The more information and support you have the easier it will be for you to offer appropriate help to your son or daughter.

SEEKING HELP

Don't hesitate to ask for help if you feel that something is wrong even if you are not sure what it is. You know your own child and should trust your own instincts. Moreover, problems that can be sorted out at an early stage are usually much easier to deal with than those that have persisted for some time. If the young person is unwilling to discuss the matter, then seek advice yourself on how best to handle the situation.

You may well feel isolated and vulnerable and blame yourself quite unnecessarily for your son or daughter's difficulties. Finding the right kind of support, even if it is simply talking to someone who understands, will help you to feel less alone and enable you to cope with the situation in a more positive way. You may find it reassuring to share your anxieties with parents who have undergone similar experiences. Talking to other parents can help you realise just how frequent such difficulties really are.

Sometimes your daughter or son may seek help from an outside source, or from a trusted friend or relative, rather than confiding in you first. Try not to feel hurt if this occurs. This is a time when independence is particularly important and they may not wish to distress you by disclosing their true feelings or they may prefer to keep their feelings to themselves. Your support will still be crucial. All young people need to know that their parents are always there for them and that they are ready to listen should they wish to talk.

You may need to be very persistent to find the help you need either for your son or daughter or for yourself. Be prepared to press for referrals or second opinions, if necessary, and contact any helpful organisations (see Chapter 15). Sometimes advice and support from one person such as an understanding GP may be enough but in many cases help from a variety of sources will make it easier to cope with different aspects of the problem. For some parents, unfortunately, it may sometimes seem as if there is no one who can offer appropriate help. But it is vital never to give up. Although you may have to search or even fight very hard to obtain it there is nearly always some suitable help available.

INFORMATION

You will find it useful to have as much relevant information as you can on the problems which may be affecting your son or daughter. This will give you greater confidence in discussing the situation either with the young person or with others who may be involved, and it will enable you to offer appropriate encouragement and support. It may also help you to feel less panicky and more in control of your own feelings and reactions. Professionals and voluntary organisations may be able to provide you with some information or suggest relevant books or leaflets, or your library or local bookshop may be able to advise. Television and radio programmes are often a good source of information. However, it is important to remember that however balanced the person producing the information is, they will always be influenced by their own point of view. You will need to look at information from a number of different sources in order to get a full picture of the situation.

SERVICES

It is generally agreed that services for young people with mental health problems or other stresses are very inadequate. Those which do exist are provided by many different agencies and vary greatly from place to place. A service that functions well in one area may be non-existent in another or extremely overstretched. Support for parents may be similarly patchy.

It may take you some time to sort out just what is available in your particular area but it is crucial to have this information so that you or your son or daughter can make the best use of what exists either now or at some future date. Without this knowledge your son or daughter could slip through the net or find that the only help offered is inappropriate.

Be prepared to make the enquiries yourself. Professionals may not have a complete picture of everything on offer or may forget to give the information unless you ask. Organisations such as Young Minds, your local citizens advice bureau, community health council or MIND group may be good starting points (see Chapter 15).

You are bound to encounter some confusion about who should provide what. Social services, the health service and education departments, all of which provide services for young people, are undergoing major organisational changes and there have been important recent changes in the law which affect young people and their families (see Chapter 14). Although ideally agencies should work together to provide the most appropriate help for the young person concerned, in practice this often fails to happen due to lack of communication or pressure of work.

You may find matters are further complicated by the fact that different services have different age limits, which in some cases vary from area to area. Younger adolescents may be catered for by services for children and young people. Older adolescents however, may fall between two stools. They may be too old for such services yet adult services may be equally inappropriate for this age group. In such cases it is important that you press for them to see a professional who has a good knowledge and understanding of young people (see Chapter 9). You also need to remember that in some instances the legal situation for young people below the age of 16 differs from that of young people aged between 16 and 18 and again from that of young people aged 18 and over (see Chapter 14).

Finally you need to be aware that your son or daughter could be offered very different help or treatment for the same problem by different agencies, according to whether their first contact is for example with social services, health, education or in some cases the courts. If what is offered seems inappropriate to you, you may need to press for other agencies to be consulted.

CHAPTER 9

Approaching Professionals

The professionals described in this chapter are those most likely to be able to offer advice, support or various forms of treatment that may be helpful to your son or daughter. Many professionals in the mental health field work as part of a team or in close contact with each other. Different professional workers have different skills and training, though quite often their roles may overlap.

A professional may offer specific treatments or suggest commonsense strategies or other sources of help. They may also offer advice and support to enable you or your son or daughter to adjust to new or unexpected situations, cope with uncertainty or draw on your own strengths and resources. It may not be possible for a professional to tackle all aspects of a problem but sometimes help in one area can increase feelings of confidence and enable changes in other areas to take place.

It is quite normal to feel nervous before you consult a professional for the first time but they should do their best to put you at ease. They should listen carefully to what you have to say and give the problem their full attention. Do not worry if your explanations are rather confused. You know your own child and will often recognise intuitively that something is wrong even if you are not quite sure what it is. Talking things through with a professional may help you to see the problem in a clearer light.

Wherever possible it is important to consult a professional who has knowledge and experience of young people and who is aware that they are often quite uncommunicative with adults about themselves. Such a professional, who is familiar with the changes and uncertainties which commonly occur in adolescence, is more likely to be able to identify real difficulties and less likely to dismiss quite worrying behaviour as just part of growing up.

Sometimes parents or young people set their hopes too high and feel disappointed because professionals cannot provide an immediate solution. Although some difficulties can be sorted out reasonably quickly once they have been identified, others are quite complex and a considerable amount of time and a variety of approaches may be needed before an improvement takes place. This does not mean that professionals will not be able to help to the best of their abilities but it does mean that there may be no quick or easy answer.

Differing views

You should not be surprised to find that there are many different views and approaches even within the same profession. This is because professionals have to find their own ways to work with people who have a range of mental health problems and stresses that are not yet fully understood. Try to remain as flexible and open-minded as you can; different approaches can often help in different ways. However, if after thinking very carefully about any explanation or suggestion you are offered or after trying out an approach, it does not seem appropriate to you or your son or daughter, say so and why, so that you can all begin to look at other possibilities.

Theories about mental health tend to a come in and out of fashion and professionals should not push any particular theory at you or your son or daughter. If they do you will have to use your own judgement to decide whether it helps to make sense of the situation for you or not. Such theories sometimes aid our understanding but they are rarely the whole truth. You also need to be aware that some professionals may present their opinions with such an air of authority that they may sound like certainties rather than the suggestions they really are.

You may, of course, be unlucky and encounter a professional who seems to have little sympathy for either you or your son or daughter. It may be that they do not seem to listen to what you have to say or that they seem intent on fitting you all into some theory rather than seeing you as individuals. You may feel that they are judging you unfairly or brushing you aside as over-anxious or insisting that everything is fine when all your instincts tell you that this is not the case. You should try to discuss your differences with the professional concerned, but if after doing so the situation remains unchanged you must have confidence in your own experience as a parent and what you know of your child. You have the right to press for appropriate help, even if this means asking for a second opinion or approaching a different agency.

Jargon

Always ask professionals to explain themselves in everyday language if there is a word or phrase you do not understand, and if the explanation is still unclear, ask them to give you a concrete example. Specialists in all fields are often lazy about using terms and expecting others to understand them, although there is no reason why you should be at all familiar with their jargon. This is particularly the case in the mental health field where different professionals may use the same term to mean different things or an ordinary word may have different meaning in a mental health context. It is in everyone's interest that explanations should be clear and you will be helping others if you point out the difficulties. This is especially important as terms which are not fully understood can make us feel even more anxious and confused. You will probably find that words seem much less threatening once their meaning is apparent.

Language and culture

If English is not your first language you may need someone to interpret for you or to speak on your behalf. Such a person needs to be familiar with your background and understand how the services operate. The professionals concerned, the citizens advice bureau or one of your own community organisations may be able to put you in touch with an interpreter, link worker or advocate. It is not advisable to use one of your children or any other close family member, as they may be too emotionally involved or upset by what is being discussed to provide clear explanations.

People in this country come from a variety of ethnic, cultural and social backgrounds. Certain situations or ways of expressing emotion which may be quite acceptable within one community may be misunderstood by a professional worker from a different background and an inappropriate course of action suggested as a result. It is important therefore to make sure that professionals have relevant information about your culture, beliefs and ways of tackling difficulties so that you can work together to support your son or daughter in the most appropriate way.

Written back-up

It is a good idea to keep copies of any letters that you send and a record of any discussions with professionals, whether over the phone or face to face. Note down who you spoke to and when, and the main points of the conversation. It is often difficult to remember exactly what people have said when you are very anxious or to be sure that you have completely understood. If you have it in writing it is easier to check back and make sure or to sort out your own views if you find that you are getting conflicting advice. It is also easy to forget the questions you wanted to ask if there is not much time for the discussion. It may help to jot them down beforehand. Having them in front of you can often give you the confidence to be a little more persistent.

Confidentiality

Both you and your son or daughter have the right to expect that discussions of a personal nature with a professional should as far as possible be kept confidential, although they may be shared with members of the team on a confidential basis. However, if you have any worries about this it is sensible to discuss them with the professional concerned to clarify the situation. This may be important if there are items of information or feelings that you do not wish to be revealed to your son or daughter in general discussion, or which they do not wish to be disclosed to you. Professionals should respect each person's right to confidentiality, although they may try to persuade families to be as open and honest with each other as they can. Professionals should, however, make it clear at the outset that in some circumstances they may not be able to keep confidentiality, for example in situations involving sexual abuse or where there is a very real risk of suicide or harm to others.

Complaints

If you have a complaint always try to talk it over with the professional concerned. You may find there has simply been a misunderstanding or you may be satisfied with an apology. If you are unable to sort it out and want to take it further it may help to get advice on the correct procedure from an organisation such as a citizens advice bureau or community health council (see Chapter 15) since making a complaint can sometimes be quite complex (see also Chapter 14). Always keep copies of all your correspondence.

Private consultation

If you are thinking of consulting a professional privately or arranging for your son or daughter to see someone on a private basis do make careful enquiries first. Find out whether that particular person has experience in dealing with your son or daughter's type of problem and whether they are used to working with young people. Check on their credentials. At present anyone can call themselves a psychologist, a psychotherapist or counsellor, for example. A recommendation from an appropriate organisation or from someone you trust is probably the safest way to start. Always check on fees beforehand, as these can vary very considerably. (To contact a consultant psychiatrist, educational or clinical psychologist or psychotherapist or counsellor privately, see Chapter 15.)

GENERAL PRACTITIONER (GP)

If your son or daughter seems very anxious or depressed, if they have inexplicable aches and pains, or if their behaviour has changed in a worrying way, for example, try to persuade them to see the GP as soon as possible. Problems are nearly always easier to sort out in the early stages.

GPs are concerned with the physical, psychological and social aspects of their patients' health and see patients in the community with a very wide range of problems. GPs will either treat patients themselves or refer them for specialist care or to other sources of help. A letter from a GP is needed for a referral to a specialist.

As a first step the GP may give the young person a physical examination and perform tests, if appropriate, to see whether a physical condition such as an illness may be contributing to their problems or whether any aches or pains have a physical cause. However, GPs are well aware that mind and body interact closely and that physical symptoms are often a way of expressing anxiety and other forms of distress. If no physical cause can be found the GP is likely to spend time talking to the young person about their feelings and about what is going on in their lives, to try and identify the problem and decide how best to deal with it.

The GP may suggest discussing the situation together with the parents, if the young person agrees. They may offer to see the young person on a regular basis to offer support, or refer them for more specialist help and advice, for example. Occasionally they may suggest prescribing drugs (see Chapter 13). If the GP does not suggest it the young person or their parents can ask for a referral to other services.

Everyone has the right to be registered with a general practitioner and young people are usually registered with their parents' GP. However they may be unwilling to go to the family GP for a number of reasons. Perhaps they are embarrassed to disclose their feelings to someone who has seen them grow up, or to someone whom they perceive as an ally of their parents, or perhaps they think that the GP is not someone they could talk to. In that case you might suggest that they see someone else in the practice, particularly if there is a doctor known to be interested in young people's problems. As a last resort, or if you are unable to get the help you need, you might consider registering with another practice. At the age of 16 a young person can register with a doctor of their choice, providing that doctor will take them.

Even if you cannot persuade your son or daughter to see a GP it is usually a good idea to see your GP yourself. Ask if you can have a longer appointment as you will need time to discuss the situation properly. The GP may be able to offer support to help you cope. They may also be able to suggest other sources of help that your daughter or son may find acceptable. If English is not your first language, ask the surgery if an interpreter is available.

Confidentiality is an important issue for parents and for young people, particularly when they have the same GP. As already explained, the GP will not disclose your anxieties to your son or daughter unless you agree. Neither will they disclose what the young person has said to them in confidence unless their safety is at risk. However, they are likely to encourage young people, particularly those under 16, to bring their difficulties out in the open and share them with their family, wherever this is appropriate.

Don't be afraid to ask questions or make suggestions. The GP won't have all the answers but should be prepared to work through the problems with you or refer you to other sources of help.

PSYCHIATRIST

Young people often worry quite unnecessarily if a referral to a psychiatrist is suggested. This may be because they mistakenly believe that psychiatrists only deal with people who are very seriously disturbed or that they admit all their patients to hospital. If so they will need reassuring that this is not the case. Psychiatrists see people with a very wide range of problems, and only a tiny minority of young people are ever admitted to hospital and then usually only after a long period of deliberation and consultation with all concerned.

Psychiatrists are qualified medical doctors who have completed further specialist training in assessing and treating a variety of mental health problems. In addition they may have further specialist skills in certain forms of treatment such as family or behaviour therapy, or a particular interest in certain fields such as eating difficulties or addiction, for example. Some specialise further in areas such as old age psychiatry or child and adolescent psychiatry.

A consultant psychiatrist holds a senior post and will work very closely with other doctors at various stages of training in psychiatry. Even though your son or daughter is referred to the consultant they may be seen by one of these doctors who will then discuss their findings and ideas for treatment with the consultant concerned. Consultant psychiatrists and those in training usually also work closely with other professional staff such as nurses, psychologists and therapists as part of a team.

Sometimes as a parent your expectations of the psychiatrist may be too high. Quite understandably you may have invested a great deal of hope in this consultation, particularly if you have been worried for some time. You need to remind yourself that the psychiatrist cannot see into your son or daughter's mind any more than you can. They have to rely on the information given to them by the young person and others and their own observations and experience in order to identify problems and suggest treatment or a course of action that may well help, but that is not a magic solution.

Child and adolescent psychiatrists

Child and adolescent psychiatrists have a specialist knowledge of the stresses that can occur as a young person changes and develops in childhood and adolescence. They generally work closely with other professionals as part of a team based at a child and adolescent clinic, although some have other posts. Whether a young person is referred to a child and adolescent clinic or to an adult psychiatrist will depend on their age and the arrangements in your particular area. In general young people up to 16 are seen at child and adolescent clinics, although some clinics may see older adolescents as well (see Chapter 11). Child and adolescent psychiatrists will usually work very closely with the young person's family in trying to sort problems out. They are much less likely to prescribe medication than adult psychiatrists.

Adult psychiatrist

Young people over 16, especially if they have left school, are more likely to be referred to an adult psychiatrist. This means that parents are less likely to be involved in their assessment and treatment. However, parents may well be asked to talk to the psychiatrist or a member of the team to help give a fuller picture of what is going on in their son or daughter's life, providing the young person is still living at home and gives their consent. Young people over 16 can make many of their own decisions about treatment and whether or not they wish their parents to be involved.

If you are worried about what is happening and have not been contacted you can ask to see the psychiatrist to discuss the problem in a general way and to find out how you can best offer support to your son or daughter. The psychiatrist may agree if it is appropriate and if they can do so without breaching confidentiality. If you feel the psychiatrist has not understood the reason for the request it may help to put it in writing. If you are still not successful you can write to the hospital manager. Your local community health council, local MIND group or SANELINE can advise (see Chapter 15).

Adult psychiatrists may suggest a range of treatments but they are far more likely to recommend medication than child and adolescent psychiatrists (see Chapter 13).

REGISTERED MENTAL NURSE (RMN)

If your son or daughter is admitted to a psychiatric ward or adolescent unit, the nurses providing care will usually be registered mental nurses who have completed a special three-year psychiatric nursing training, and those in training. They are responsible for patients 24 hours a day in a caring role and normally work very closely with other professionals as part of a team. Their observations can be particularly valuable in reaching a diagnosis or deciding on treatment. Some RMNs have had further specialist training and may offer family or group therapy, for example. They may be known as nurse therapists or clinical nurse specialists.

RMNs working on adult psychiatric wards will have a wide experience of mental health problems generally but may have had no special training or experience in working with adolescents. However, senior nurses in adolescent units are likely to have had special training in this field.

As young people see nurses throughout the day they may confide in them but they may also test their limits and vent their anger on them just as they might on parents at home. Nurses see all sides of the young person and should therefore be particularly understanding of your difficulties as a parent.

If there are any problems you need to discuss you will probably find that most nurses are approachable. They tend to be practical and down to earth and to avoid jargon. If they cannot help they should be able to suggest who can.

COMMUNITY PSYCHIATRIC NURSE (CPN)

Community psychiatric nurses are registered mental nurses who have had extra training in working in the community. They work from a variety of bases including psychiatric units, GP surgeries and community mental health centres to support people with mental health problems who are living at home, and their families.

CPNs specialising in children and adolescents generally work as part of a team at a child and adolescent clinic and may see young people and their families in that setting. Each CPN will have particular skills to offer, such as family or behaviour therapy, depending on their own interests and the needs of the team.

If your son or daughter is too old to attend a child and adolescent clinic (see Chapter 11), you may find it helpful to talk to a CPN who could visit you at home to assess the situation. Depending on where you live you may be able to approach a CPN directly or you may need a referral from the GP or consultant psychiatrist. Ask your local community health council (see Chapter 15) what system operates in your area.

HEALTH VISITOR

Health visitors are nurses who have had further training in providing information and advice on health and health services. They are particularly concerned with the well-being of the whole family and can offer emotional support as well as practical suggestions on how to cope with the stresses of family life.

You may find it helpful to talk through any worries about your son or daughter, or about what is going on at home, with someone who is familiar with the kinds of family pressure you are experiencing. You can contact a health visitor through your GP surgery or health clinic. The health visitor should be able to offer you support and suggest where you can go for further advice and help. They are unlikely to offer direct support to the young person but should be able to tell you what services exist for young people in the area.

SCHOOL NURSE

School nurses are qualified nurses with extra training in working with young people. They work full- or part-time in many schools. Parents or young people can talk to them in confidence. The school secretary will know their visiting pattern and whether you can drop in or should make an appointment. You do not have to say why you wish to see them.

A young person who finds it difficult to talk to parents or a family doctor about their problems may be able to confide in the school nurse. School nurses can offer information, advice and support to young people with a range of problems such as depression, worries about relationships or exams, being bullied or taking drugs. They will respect the young person's confidence unless they are at risk.

They may arrange to see the young person on a regular basis for support and counselling or refer them to other suitable sources of help. If the young person agrees they may talk to other people on their behalf. The nurse will try to persuade young people under 16 to include their parents in discussions at some stage. Older adolescents have the right to decide whether or not parents should be involved but the school nurse should help them to involve the most appropriate people.

Parents can contact the school nurse for advice without the young person knowing. There may be occasions when the school nurse would agree to see the young person at a parent's request.

PSYCHOTHERAPIST

Child psychotherapists who work with young people up to the age of 18 have completed a recognised training course and have extensive experience of young people's emotional difficulties. Your son or daughter may encounter a child psychotherapist at a child and adolescent clinic. Psychotherapists with a training in adult psychotherapy and a special interest in young people may also sometimes work as part of the team in child and adolescent centres, in youth counselling centres or in adult psychiatric settings for example. In addition other professionals, such as clinical psychologists, may also have a training in psychotherapy and offer it as one of their skills.

Your son or daughter may be offered individual or group psychotherapy if it is felt that it would be helpful for them to spend some time exploring their earlier feelings in order to better understand their present reactions (see Chapter 12). This may be particularly valuable with a problem that seems entrenched. Psychotherapy is quite often given alongside other sorts of therapy.

Although psychotherapists are trained in a variety of ways and have different methods of working, they will all aim to listen carefully and caringly to what the young person says and to support them in working through their problems so that they can feel more in charge of their own life and more able to make their own choices.

OCCUPATIONAL THERAPIST (OT)

Young people may come into contact with an occupational therapist if they are admitted to hospital or an adolescent unit; they may also be referred to an OT for individual or group work or for various types of therapy while living at home.

The OT will aim to help your daughter or son become more confident and independent in the outside world and will encourage them to develop those coping skills that they would have acquired naturally had they not been hampered by a mental health problem or by other stresses. The OT will look at all aspects of the young person's life in order to help them build on their strengths and deal with difficult areas.

Depending on the situation the OT may assist young people with practical skills such as shopping, cooking, budgeting, filling in forms and paying bills, or social skills such as answering the phone, attending a job interview or asking a friend for a meal. They may run groups in which young people can practise handling situations through role play, discuss ideas or learn ways to communicate more effectively. They are also likely to be involved in creative activities such as art, music, drama or movement therapy which can help increase young people's self-esteem (see Chapter 12).

The OT will encourage your daughter or son to pursue their hobbies and interests and find ways of meeting other young people. When they are ready they can help them plan ahead and support them in applying for a course or a job or in structuring their day in a more satisfying way.

SOCIAL WORKER

Social services departments are organised in different ways but they will all have social workers who are particularly concerned with children and families. Social workers also work in other settings such as hospitals, child and adolescent clinics, voluntary organisations and residential care. Social workers will, where possible, help people to help themselves by providing information, support and practical advice and by putting them in touch with other organisations where appropriate. They also have a duty to protect children at risk. They may have additional skills such as family therapy.

Social workers are trained to look at problems in the context of the family and the community. They can be very helpful in suggesting ways to deal with outside pressures and with stresses within the family itself. However, although some social workers also have additional appropriate skills, most are not trained to recognise or deal with mental health problems. So if you think it is a problem of this sort you should contact the GP.

If you want to talk over problems with a social worker in a general way you could telephone social services and ask to speak to the duty social worker or call in at your local area office. The social worker may suggest further sources of help or arrange for someone to visit the family at home to try and get a fuller picture of the situation. You can also ask for help under the Children Act (see Chapter 14). Unfortunately many social services departments are very stretched through trying to deal with suspected child abuse cases and therefore have less time and resources for other types of problem.

If there is a question of your son or daughter being detained under the Mental Health Act 1983 an Approved Social Worker (ASW) will be involved. An ASW is a qualified social worker who has been specially trained and approved by the local authority to handle mental health problems. An ASW will always look for alternatives to compulsory admission. In Scotland the equivalent of an ASW is a Mental Health Officer.

Unfortunately the term 'social worker' is sometimes used to describe both qualified and unqualified workers. The vast majority of social workers working in local authority departments or health settings are trained, but only a minority of residential social workers have qualifications at present.

CLINICAL PSYCHOLOGIST

Clinical psychologists have a degree in psychology, which includes the study of normal and abnormal behaviour, followed by a further qualification in assessing and treating people's emotional and psychological problems. They have a range of skills which they can draw on as appropriate. These may include family, behaviour, and group therapy, cognitive behaviour therapy, social skills training and counselling or psychotherapy (see Chapter 12). Some clinical psychologists specialise in children and adolescents.

Clinical psychologists may also be involved in assessing people's abilities in a variety of ways to help them use their strengths to the best advantage and overcome their difficulties. Your son or daughter should not be surprised if they are given a questionnaire to fill in at the first interview or if they are asked to record information about their thoughts, feelings and behaviour during the following weeks.

If your son or daughter is referred to a child and adolescent clinic or psychiatric unit they might be seen by a clinical psychologist if appropriate. However, they could also be referred directly to a clinical psychologist. You can ask the GP for a referral if you feel it might be helpful. In some places referrals from other professionals or self-referrals are accepted. Your GP surgery or community health council (see Chapter 15) should be able to tell you which system operates in your area. Whether or not your son or daughter will see a clinical psychologist who specialises in children and adolescents may depend on where you live.

EDUCATIONAL PSYCHOLOGIST

Educational psychologists have a degree in psychology and an additional qualification in educational psychology as well as being trained teachers with a minimum of two years' teaching experience. They aim to help sort out problems that seem to be related to young people's own development and to school. These may include behaviour problems at school, learning difficulties, anxieties about schoolwork and school refusal. The educational psychologist may work with parents, or schools or with the young person directly, depending on the situation. Your permission as a parent will always be asked before your son or daughter is seen.

Young people, parents and teachers may all find it easier to talk frankly to someone who is both outside the school and the family and who is likely therefore to have a more objective view. The educational psychologist may be able to suggest new ways of tackling the problem which all those concerned are prepared to try. Often small changes are enough to help the young person to feel more understood and supported and improve the situation. Sometimes, however, the young person may need further specialist help and the educational psychologist can advise on this.

If your son or daughter is not performing well at school and various ways of helping have been tried without success, you may decide with the educational psychologist and the school that a formal assessment of your child's education needs would be a sensible step in order to provide a fuller understanding of the problem and appropriate provision to meet their needs (see Chapter 14). If the school does not suggest consulting an educational psychologist and you feel that their advice might be helpful, ask the school if this can be arranged. In some areas you can get in touch with an educational psychologist direct. Your education authority will tell you how. Your education authority will be listed under the name of your local authority in the telephone book.

EDUCATION WELFARE OFFICER (EWO)

Education welfare officers, also known in some areas as education social workers (ESWs), provide help for young people who are having difficulties that affect their schooling. They may be missing school, falling behind with their work, or exhibiting emotional or behavioural problems at school, for example. Referrals may come from schools, from other organisations, from parents or from young people themselves.

Depending on the situation, the education welfare officer may talk to the young person, or the parents, or both, either at school, or at home or at the education office, if preferred. They will spend some time in trying to find out what the problem is and what is causing it. Causes may include anxieties due to family problems, bullying, difficulties with a particular teacher or pressures from the peer group.

Ways of dealing with the problem that the education welfare officer might suggest could include meeting teachers to enlist their support, sessions with the family to help them find ways to improve the situation, and referral to other sources of support. They will also offer practical advice on welfare benefits, for example, or on ways to help a young person gradually return to school.

You can contact an education welfare officer via your son or daughter's school or through your education authority, which is listed under the name of your local authority in the telephone book.

CHAPTER 10

Consultation with Professionals

Your daughter or son's distress or changed behaviour may be due to a combination of different factors and you yourself may not always be clear just why you feel something is not quite right. Any professionals you consult will need a considerable amount of background information in order to try to understand what the problem actually is and what some of the causes may be, before they can suggest an appropriate course of action. You should not be surprised therefore if professionals ask a great many questions at the first, and perhaps second interview, as well as listening to what you have to say.

Of course, different professionals will approach problems in different ways, according to their skills and training, but many of the questions may be similar. If you see several professionals you may well find that you are going over the same ground again so try to be patient and don't be afraid to ask questions yourself or contribute your own thoughts and observations, where appropriate.

If you and your family come from a very different background from the professionals you are seeing it is important to make sure that they have enough information to understand your beliefs and your way of life so that they can see your daughter or son's problems in context. If you have been brought up to behave in a respectful and unquestioning way towards professionals you may find it hard to ask questions or explain your own point of view, but it is important to do so in order to try and sort out what is best for the young person. If English is not your first language you may need help from an interpreter or link worker. Ask if one can be provided.

Whether young people are seen separately or with their family may depend on their age and circumstances and the particular professional's way of working. Sometimes a professional may see you all together or separately and then together, sometimes they may simply see your daughter or son, and sometimes, where the young person is unwilling to seek help, they may see parents on their own.

The professional may ask permission to contact other people who may be able to contribute information or observations, such as a teacher or social worker. Up to the age of 16 the parent and the young person will be involved in deciding whether to give consent for this. After the age of 16 young people can usually give or withhold consent themselves (see Chapter 14).

You, or your daughter or son, may feel nervous before a first meeting with a professional but they should do their best to put you at ease. Try to be as frank as you can in explaining your concerns and in answering questions, even if you do not understand their relevance immediately. The aim of the meeting is to help everyone to understand the problem more fully, not to catch anyone out or apportion blame. Some questions will be asked to see whether certain factors can be excluded as possible causes of the distress and others to build up a general picture of the situation. Your daughter or son may find it reassuring to know the sorts of question that might be asked. You will have to use your judgement to decide whether it would be helpful to discuss these with them in a general way beforehand.

If the person interviewing is a doctor, your son or daughter may be given a physical examination or various tests to check on the possibility of a physical illness. They will probably be asked about any medication they may be taking, whether prescribed or over the counter, and may be asked whether they smoke, drink alcohol or take illicit drugs. You should not feel upset if your son or daughter is asked these questions. They are asked as a matter of routine.

At the end of an interview, or several interviews, the professional should try and clarify the problem, or an aspect of the problem, with those concerned and discuss possible ways of dealing with it. This may be through further meetings, for example, through some form of therapy, through advice and help from another source, through commonsense suggestions or through a decision to simply wait and see.

QUESTIONS FOR THE FAMILY

It is very common for all members of the family who are living at home to be invited to the first and perhaps second interview at a child and adolescent clinic (see Chapter 11). Other professionals may sometimes want to see the whole family as well. Families play such a large part in the lives of young people that it is helpful to look at the problem in the context of the whole family and to find out everyone's point of view. It is also easier to enlist each family member's support if they are involved at the start. If they do not understand the situation or feel excluded in some way they may undermine the young person's confidence in whatever course of action is suggested.

Each member of the family, including the young person, may be asked how they are affected by the situation and how they try to deal with it. Each family member may also be asked about both upsetting and positive experiences in their life, about their views of the present and their expectations for the future. There are also likely to be questions about stresses affecting the whole family such as unemployment, ill-health, or a separation or divorce, and about whether there is a history of physical or psychological illness in the family. Parents may be asked about their own adolescence and this may help them to begin to think about how their own experiences may be influencing their expectations of their son or daughter.

The professional is trying to build up a picture of your family in order to understand the stresses or attitudes that may be contributing to the problem and in order to identify the strengths you can all draw on to deal with the situation, either on your own or with some support.

Seeing how people interact as a family can also help the professional to suggest the most appropriate form of treatment. Family members too can benefit. Each person will be aware of rather different aspects of the situation. The family meeting gives them a chance to share their anxieties, pool their observations and correct each other's misunderstandings. Sometimes it quickly becomes apparent that the real difficulty is rather different to the one everyone imagined, and quite often families can suggest their own ways to sort things out. It is very important therefore that everyone makes the effort to attend a family meeting, even if it means taking time off work or school.

It is quite common for other professionals working as a team to observe the family meeting through one-way screens or video. This is to make sure that nothing important is missed and to offer additional skills in sorting out what the difficulties are and what course of action might be appropriate. Your consent to this should be asked before the meeting. If you have any reservations, discuss these with your therapist.

QUESTIONS FOR THE YOUNG PERSON

Your son or daughter is likely to be asked about their feelings and what they think the problem might be, if indeed they believe there is a problem. There are likely to be questions on their upbringing and family relationships, their situation at work or school, their friendships and interests and their plans for the future. The professional is trying to find out what sort of person they are when they are not under stress. They may also ask about worries or disappointments in the past or present, about anxieties over sex or relationships, if appropriate, and about things they like or dislike about themselves. They may be asked about any changes in their sleeping or eating patterns, their weight, their level of energy or their ability to concentrate, for example, to see how the problem may be affecting them and what sort of help might be needed.

Older adolescents are likely to prefer seeing a professional on their own in order to preserve their privacy. Depending on the young person's age and circumstances and their agreement, the professional concerned may well wish to see other members of the family to gain a fuller understanding of the situation.

QUESTIONS FOR PARENTS

As a parent you may be asked for details about your son or daughter's early development that they will be unable to remember. These may range from their sleeping and feeding habits in the early months to whether they played happily as a toddler or settled down easily at school. You will probably also be asked for observations about their later childhood and adolescence, including their progress at school, their friendships, their interests and enthusiasms, and their general confidence. The professional may also want details about their health and any illnesses, accidents or allergies, for example. All this information may help to establish when the problem may have started and what, up till now, the young person has found easy or difficult to cope with. Finally, you may be asked about any changes you have noticed in your son or daughter's recent moods, habits or behaviour that may have caused you concern.

If your son or daughter is unwilling to seek help you may see a professional yourself for support and advice on how best to handle the situation. As the young person is not there to speak for themselves you are likely to be asked a great many questions about their symptoms and the changes in their behaviour. It may help to write down certain points beforehand such as when you first noticed the difficulties or changes occurring, what form they took and why you find them particularly worrying.

CHAPTER 11

Unfamiliar Settings

Advice and help may be offered in a variety of places depending on the organisation concerned and the arrangements in each particular area. Such places might include the GP surgery or health centre, your own home, local authority offices, your son or daughter's school, a child and adolescent clinic, an adolescent unit, a residential home, a voluntary organisation, or a hospital psychiatric department, for example.

Most people feel a little anxious when visiting a place for the first time, especially if it is hard to find or they are not sure what the procedures are. If you are not familiar with the setting it may help you, or your son or daughter, to feel more confident if you telephone beforehand to ask for exact directions and to find out details such as who to ask for on arrival, likely waiting times or how long the interview will take. If English is not your first language you may want to ask about interpreting services or whether you can bring someone from your own community to help with explanations.

Although there is not space to describe every type of setting and although settings themselves vary greatly according to local arrangements and circumstances, the following descriptions may give you some idea of what to expect.

CHILD AND ADOLESCENT CLINICS

There is likely to be at least one community or hospital-based child and adolescent clinic in your health district, though it may be known under a different name such as a child and family consultation centre, family and young persons unit, family counselling services or child guidance clinic. These clinics generally see young people up to the age of 16, usually with their families but occasionally on their own. Some clinics will also see young people up to 17 or 18 if they are still at school and living at home, or if they have been seen by the clinic before. Most clinics will also see parents on their own.

All child and adolescent clinics deal with a wide range of problems from the mildly worrying to the more severe and you will usually be referred to the one nearest your home by your GP, or sometimes by another professional. If your GP does not suggest a referral you can ask for one. In some areas you can refer yourself.

Clinics are staffed by a team of professionals, sometimes known as the child mental health team, which varies in composition from clinic to clinic but which usually includes a child and adolescent psychiatrist. Among the other professionals who might help to make up the team are a clinical psychologist, a child psychotherapist, a social worker specialising in children and families, a community psychiatric nurse specialising in children and adolescents, an educational psychologist and an art or drama therapist.

Which professional you see will depend on individual arrangements at particular clinics. In some clinics the whole team will discuss referrals and allocate each one to the professional with the most relevant skills. In other clinics the consultant child and adolescent psychiatrist, or junior doctor in training, will see all referrals initially and then pass them on to other team members as appropriate. Each professional will draw on the help and expertise of other team members as required.

Child and adolescent clinics aim to help young people and their families find their own strengths and confidence to deal with situations in the way that seems best for all concerned. Support and help may range from the opportunity to talk through problems and possible courses of action to a variety of therapies. These may include individual, group and family therapy, behaviour and cognitive behaviour therapy, social skills training and art and drama therapy (see Chapter 12). Medication may occasionally be advised. Families may be encouraged to make use of other resources in the area ranging from counselling to recreational activities, as appropriate.

If you want information on your local child and adolescent clinic ask your GP, citizens advice bureau or Young Minds (see Chapter 15), or telephone the clinic itself. Waiting times for appointments do vary. If you have already been referred to a clinic and are worried about how to manage until you are seen, you could ask to speak to the professional to whom you have been allocated about how best to deal with the situation.

ADOLESCENT UNITS

Young people and their families will normally only be referred to a health service adolescent unit for assessment and treatment after a number of professionals have been seen and various courses of action have been tried without success. These units, which are few and far between, usually offer outpatient treatment as well as some residential and day places. Units vary considerably in approach, the type of problem they deal with and the range of treatments offered. They may cater for young people between 12 and 19, or a narrower age band, depending on their own arrangements.

If a young person is referred to an adolescent unit, professionals will usually work with them and their family on an outpatient basis to try and sort things out. It is obviously preferable that a young person should remain at home, in familiar surroundings and among their own friends, wherever possible. If more help is needed they may sometimes be invited to attend the unit on a day basis. Admission to residential care, which offers the opportunity for more intensive assessment and treatment and for nursing care, will normally be planned and will only take place after careful consideration by those concerned, including the young person and their family. Most adolescent units have teachers attached to them. Staff will continue to work with families, while young people are in the unit, and visits home may be arranged where appropriate.

If you would like information on your nearest adolescent units contact Young Minds (see Chapter 15). If you or your son or daughter are worried about any aspect of care or treatment, or have a complaint that you are unable to sort out, your local community health council, MIND group or SANELINE should be able to advise (see Chapter 15).

ADULT PSYCHIATRY OUTPATIENTS

If your daughter or son is over 16 and has left school, they are more likely to be referred by their GP to an adult psychiatric clinic than to a child and family clinic.

It is widely recognised that this group of young people is poorly provided for. Although young people themselves may appreciate the greater privacy offered by adult psychiatry, adult psychiatric settings are not on the whole very suitable environments for distressed young people. Moreover, adult psychiatrists in general will not have the same knowledge of the developmental problems of adolescence as child and adolescent psychiatrists, although individual psychiatrists may well have a good understanding of young people. In addition, as with any branch of medicine, different mental health teams may hold very different views on methods of treatment. If you or your son or daughter are unhappy with the advice or treatment offered you could ask for a second opinion or you could ask the psychiatrist concerned to discuss the problem with a child and adolescent psychiatrist, or ask your GP to suggest this.

Once your son or daughter has been referred they will usually be sent an appointment to see the consultant psychiatrist or one of the junior doctors in training in outpatients (see Chapter 9). You may want to accompany your son or daughter to the first appointment to give them support but do not be offended if they prefer to go alone or take a friend. The interview will probably last about an hour.

The doctor concerned may ask your son or daughter's permission to talk to members of their family or to other professionals. They may arrange to see the young person again or refer them for treatment to other members of the team, or suggest other sources of help or courses of action. They will write explaining their recommendations to the young person's GP.

ADULT PSYCHIATRIC WARD

Only a small number of young people are admitted to a psychiatric ward. A psychiatrist might wish to admit a young person in order to carry out a thorough assessment before deciding on treatment, for example. Young people might also be admitted if they needed constant support and monitoring, or if they were so distressed or disturbed that hospital care seemed to be the best option.

Nearly all young people who are admitted will be admitted as voluntary patients. This means that if they are 16 or over they will have talked the matter over with their doctor and agreed to come in of their own free will. If they are below the age of 16 parents are likely to be involved in discussions on admission and treatment but the young person should still be consulted (see Chapter 14). Any young person under 16 should be seen by a member of the child mental health team and every effort made to find an alternative bed in a more appropriate ward as soon as possible.

Very occasionally a young person may be compulsorily detained in hospital under the 1983 Mental Health Act. The situation is then rather different, but they will still have certain important rights (see Chapter 14).

Information about the hospital, including details such as visiting times, should be sent to your son or daughter or given to them on admission. Apart from the individual treatment that your son or daughter will receive, there is likely to be a weekly programme of activities as part of the overall treatment plan. Such activities may include group discussions, art therapy, cookery and social skills, for example.

You will probably have very mixed feelings if your son or daughter goes into hospital. For example you may feel relieved that someone else will be caring for them for a time, but also very anxious about whether everything is being done for the best. Moreover, if you have shouldered most of the responsibility for your son or daughter over a very worrying period you may also feel rather excluded from what is going on.

Although professionals have to keep confidentiality it is obviously important that you are able to talk freely to the consultant or to one of the other members of the team about your own anxieties and ways in which you can best help your son or daughter. If you experience difficulties in doing so your local community health council, MIND group or SANELINE can advise (see Chapter 15).

You may find it very upsetting to see your son or daughter in hospital and you may dread visiting because you know you have to leave them there. However, it is important to visit regularly and to encourage others to do so or to send letters or cards. Even if you are met with a hostile or apathetic response you are showing that you still care and helping to maintain the links with the young person's ordinary life. As they improve you may be able to take them out for a meal or home for the weekend.

Occasionally, however, staff may wish to limit visiting in order to try out a new approach. Perhaps you have had to be so supportive as a family that the young person has become too dependent on you and needs a little space. If you are not happy with the explanation given ask to speak to your son or daughter's consultant or to the nurse who has particular responsibility for their care.

A care plan should be worked out before your son or daughter is discharged from hospital. This should include a named person for them to contact. Ask if you can talk over the care plan with the staff concerned so that you will be able to offer support and know what to do in a crisis.

If you or your son or daughter are unhappy about any aspects of care or treatment and you are unable to sort this out informally by talking to the staff or the consultant concerned, ask to see the hospital's complaints procedure. Advice on making a complaint can be obtained from the hospital manager and from your local community health council, MIND group or SANELINE (see Chapter 15).

EMERGENCY HOSPITAL ADMISSION

If your daughter or son is taken to hospital in an emergency, for example after an overdose, they may be admitted to a paediatric ward or an adult medical or psychiatric ward, depending on their age, the hospital's policy and the availability of beds. You will obviously be very distressed but it is important to do all you can to make sure your daughter or son sees an appropriate professional who can discuss the situation with them and set up some form of help before they leave hospital. Up to the age of 16, or in some cases leaving school if this is later, your son or daughter should be seen by a member of the child mental health team. Older adolescents or those who have left school should be seen by a member of the adult psychiatric team.

RESIDENTIAL HOMES AND SCHOOLS

If arrangements are being made for your son or daughter to live away from home in a residential home or boarding school, for example, then it is very important to check on the qualifications and experience of those who will be caring for them as well as those who will be teaching them. You will also need to ask about matters such as staffing levels and staff turnover, as well as about the rules, routine, and arrangements for visits. Answers to specific questions will probably give you a clearer idea about the place than replies to general enquiries about policy or aims, which can always be made to sound impressive. It is also a good idea to ask to see copies of the latest Inspection Reports.

If your child has been statemented as having special needs under the 1993 Education Act (see Chapter 14), then they will need teachers who are skilled in dealing with their particular problem. You should make sure that there are sufficient teachers at the school to give them individual attention for some of the time and to enable them to work in small groups.

Wherever possible you should visit to see for yourself and talk to as many people there as you can, including young people. It is important that you should feel that the head of home or school is someone who is easily approachable, that there is a friendly, open atmosphere and that there is a recognised complaints procedure through which young people and parents can make informal and formal complaints that can be independently investigated. Professionals can sometimes seem rather intimidating, but remember you are still responsible for your son or daughter, even while they are not living at home. You therefore have every right to make thorough enquiries. If your questions are brushed aside or you are unable to look round freely you should think very carefully before agreeing to that particular establishment.

Residential homes and boarding schools vary greatly in quality. A good home or school can provide a young person with a period of stability and support and a chance to patch up relationships with their family, if these have deteriorated. They can also give your daughter or son the opportunity to benefit from new relationships with staff and other young people. A badly run home or school which is inadequately staffed or where there is constant friction, bullying or a general feeling of apathy, for example, may make it even more difficult for the young person to cope.

It is very important to keep in regular contact with your son or daughter, whatever the difficulties may be. Being away from home and friends can be a very lonely experience and your support will still be crucial in helping them to cope. It is also important to keep in touch with the home or school, either through contact with the head, or with a member of staff who has special responsibility for your son or daughter, and to attend regular reviews, parents' meetings or any school functions to give your child support.

If you have any worries about your son or daughter try to sort them out through the established complaints procedure. The Children's Legal Centre can advise on problems relating to both education and care. ACE can advise on problems relating to education. The Family Rights Group can advise on problems relating to care if your son or daughter is in social services care or accommodation, or they themselves can ring NAYPIC (see Chapter 15).

YOUTH COUNSELLING, ADVICE AND INFORMATION CENTRES

These centres, run by a variety of organisations, cater for young people, usually between the ages of 13 and 25. They offer different kinds of services so you or your son or daughter may want to make some enquiries first. Some centres offer support and help on specific issues such as drug problems, for example, while others may deal with a wide range of problems or offer counselling or psychotherapy. Staff will have experience in dealing with young people, and older adolescents in particular may prefer to use such a service as it offers them more privacy and independence as parents are not involved. Centres are likely to be friendly and informal and encourage young people to drop in and discuss their difficulties, which will be treated in complete confidence. Information, advice or counselling may be offered, depending on the centre, and other sources of help may be suggested. For details of your nearest centre contact Youth Access or Young Minds or ask your GP, citizens advice bureau or library (see Chapter 15).

CHAPTER 12

A Range of Therapies

Therapy is another word for treatment and this chapter describes some of the therapies which may be offered to your daughter or son or to your family. These may be based on talking and listening, on learning new skills or responses, or on practical or creative approaches. All these treatments involve helping people to help themselves. The following chapter describes treatment involving medication. Before embarking on a particular treatment the therapist should agree some general aims with your daughter or son, and with you, if appropriate, and explain just what the treatment involves.

Each young person is of course an individual and their particular circumstances are unique. This means that the factors that contribute to mental health problems and stresses, and the reactions to these factors, will vary from person to person. It is therefore difficult to predict exactly how your son or daughter may respond to a particular therapy or therapist or to various practical suggestions. Quite often a number of different approaches will be suggested to tackle different aspects of the problem.

You may feel rather defensive if some sort of therapy is suggested but you should not see this as a criticism of either you as a parent, or of your daughter or son. Therapists have skills and experience in helping people to work through problems that they would find difficult to deal with on their own. In addition it is often easier for young people to talk to someone outside the family about their anxieties rather than to someone close. However, you are still your son or daughter's most important source of support.

Adolescence can be a very confusing time and many young people need some help in coping with pressures or in managing to become more independent. But it can sometimes be very hard for parents to disentangle just what is happening when their own daughter or son is troubled, especially if the young person is uncommunicative. Knowing that a therapist is there to offer them support may go some way towards relieving your worry. It can also enable you to step back a little and allow your daughter or son more space.

However, it is important to remember that motivation is essential. The young person, and their family, must want to do something about the problem and must be open to change. If your daughter or son is unwilling to accept any type of therapy at present then you may have to be patient. They may be more receptive at a later date. In the mean time seek help for yourself on how best to offer them support and deal with the situation.

One of the aims of therapy is to raise people's confidence and self-esteem so that they can draw on their own strengths and resources. Therapy should help your daughter or son find out more about themselves so that they can make the kinds of choices that they feel comfortable with at that particular time. Of course these may not necessarily be the choices you would have made for them but part of growing up is learning to take your own decisions and learning to deal with your own mistakes.

Therapy is rarely an instant or a complete solution but it can help to make many difficulties more manageable. Although in some cases you may notice a rapid improvement in your daughter or son's well-being or their ability to cope, in many cases changes may be quite gradual. But even small, positive steps are encouraging. Young people often feel trapped or boxed in by their own expectations, or the expectations of those around them, especially when they are anxious or distressed. Through therapy they may learn that there are different ways of looking at relationships and of approaching situations. This in turn can give them a feeling of freedom and a sense of being more in control of their own life.

You need to be aware that mental health problems and stresses may absorb so much of a young person's energy that they have little left for other areas such as schoolwork, for example, or relationships. This means that even when they start to improve through therapy or other means, they may still take some time to catch up with their friends. You also need to be aware that some of the changes which may take place during therapy may not always be the ones you had expected. For example, a young person who has previously been very compliant and anxious to please may become more assertive and questioning as their confidence increases. However, any signs of normal adolescent development should be welcomed even if they are a little difficult to handle at first.

You may well find that problems of your own surface while you are dealing with your son or daughter's difficulties. These may be due to tensions between you and someone close to you, for example, or they may be problems that you failed to resolve during your own adolescence. Getting help for yourself may also help you handle the situation with your son or daughter. Depending on the problem, your GP or one of the organisations listed in Chapter 15 may be able to suggest appropriate sources of help.

FAMILY THERAPY

The aim of family therapy is to encourage members of the family to work together to find their own appropriate ways of dealing with problems without attributing blame. Family therapy has been found to be one of the quickest and most effective ways of handling certain types of problem.

Difficulties and misunderstandings arise in all families from time to time. Even families who are managing well usually have at least one or two areas where they cope less effectively. In some cases unresolved problems may give rise to frequent argument; in others certain issues are carefully avoided for fear of what might occur if they were brought out into the open. Sometimes families find that ways of dealing with matters that once worked well in the past no longer do so now because family members have changed or because there are additional stresses to cope with such as illness or unemployment. Everyone may need help to adapt and find new ways of handling situations.

Before family therapy is offered you are likely to have already had one or two family meetings with a therapist in which each family member has had the opportunity to talk about themselves and explain their view of the situation (see Chapter 10). Family therapy may be suggested if it seems that it would be helpful for everyone to spend some time looking a little more closely at some of the issues that have emerged and discussing various ways to deal with them. Family therapy will not usually delve into the past or into your deeper feelings but will focus very much on what is going on at present. Its main aim is to help you all to use your own resources and find acceptable ways to cope.

Each family is different and there is no one right way to handle situations but you may find that trying a new approach can help you to become more flexible and see things in a different way. Quite often small adjustments in attitudes or behaviour may be all that is needed to help deal with a difficult situation or to meet each other's changing needs. For example, you may as a parent decide to spend more time with your son or daughter, perhaps sharing an activity you both enjoy, and this in turn may improve your relationship; or the whole family may agree to a fairer division of chores so that one or two members do not feel over-burdened and unappreciated; or you may decide that you should all have a leisurely meal together at least once a week at which everyone has the chance to talk and listen.

Sometimes it may become apparent, during the sessions, that your son or daughter's difficult behaviour is simply their way of coping with anxiety about hidden stresses in the family, such as tension between you and your partner. If these real difficulties can be acknowledged, it can lift the burden from your son or daughter. It may not be appropriate to tackle these underlying problems during family therapy but the therapist may be able to suggest other sources of help.

Family therapy can be helpful at any age. However, it is less likely to be suggested for older adolescents who are trying to establish their independence from their family and who are therefore anxious to preserve their privacy.

Sessions will probably last about an hour, and there may be one or two therapists present. There will also sometimes be a one-way screen or video so that other professionals in the team can offer their skills without being too intrusive. However, if you feel concerned about this, discuss it with your therapist. A gap of several weeks is normally left between each session to enable the family to try out any ideas that have been discussed or that have occurred to them. The number of sessions will vary but quite often five or six sessions will give everyone enough confidence to become more flexible and to find their own suitable ways of handling situations.

COUNSELLING AND PSYCHOTHERAPY

Individual counselling or psychotherapy offers people a time just for themselves in which they can explore their difficulties and feelings with the help of the therapist. This in itself can often boost self-confidence. However, young people are sometimes hesitant about embarking on a one-to-one relationship with an adult. You may need to reassure your son or daughter that the counsellor or psychotherapist is there to listen without making any judgements, and to offer them support while they work through their problems at their own pace.

Counselling and psychotherapy with young people are similar. They are both based on a knowledge of child and adolescent psychology and both lay great stress on the ways in which relationships and childhood experience help to contribute to the development of the personality. However, generally speaking, in counselling the young person will probably focus more on the problems they are experiencing at present and quite often on specific problems. With a psychotherapist, on the other hand, they are more likely to spend a considerable amount of time exploring their earlier experiences in order to try and understand the causes of their present difficulties. This approach is sometimes referred to as 'psychodynamic'.

Counsellors and psychotherapists use a number of different approaches but their aim will be to establish a relationship of trust in which the young person feels safe enough to look at their own feelings and to talk about what is troubling them. By listening attentively and through offering suggestions to help them clarify their thoughts and feelings, the therapist may be able to help the young person to gradually gain a better understanding of their own problems and of who they are and what they want from life. They can also be helped to gain a clearer picture of how they get on with people generally through understanding how they relate to their therapist.

Your son or daughter may feel upset when they disclose their real feelings for the first time or talk about their fears or anxieties, but the therapist is trained to offer appropriate support, and afterwards they will probably feel a sense of relief. Finding that the therapist takes their feelings seriously can often help to make them more manageable and fears which have been expressed usually become less frightening.

You may need to explain that the counsellor or psychotherapist is not able to provide solutions and will not usually tell them what to do. However, knowing that they are valued by the therapist as a person can help to raise your son or daughter's self-esteem. As their confidence increases they may see situations in a different light. They may realise that there are ways in which they themselves can start to tackle their problems and that there are more choices open to them in life than they had previously thought.

It may take some weeks or even months for your daughter or son to become used to the therapist and their way of working and to feel the benefit, so try to persuade them to be patient and to give it a chance. They also need to realise that counselling or psychotherapy can be an up-and-down process in which some sessions may be very helpful and others seem less so, but that it is important to continue to go on a regular basis in order to get the most benefit. Sessions, which may be weekly, usually last 50 minutes to an hour.

Counselling or psychotherapy may be offered through child and adolescent clinics or through adult psychiatry units, although there is very little provision for individual psychotherapy in the health service. It can also sometimes be arranged through education or social services. Counselling and psychotherapy may also be offered by youth counselling services or specialist agencies (see Chapter 15).

If you decide to consult a counsellor or psychotherapist privately, be sure to check on their credentials as well as fees. Anyone can set themselves up either as a counsellor or as a psychotherapist. It is best to get a recommendation from someone you trust or to check with a suitable organisation such as the British Association for Counselling or the United Kingdom Council for Psychotherapy. You might also enquire what free or low-cost counselling is available locally from professionals or trained volunteers. The citizens advice bureau or local community or religious organisations may be able to advise (see Chapter 15).

BEHAVIOUR THERAPY

Behaviour therapy can be a very effective way of overcoming specific problems such as fears, phobias and obsessions. If it is suggested for your son or daughter you may need to reassure them that it is a straightforward and practical approach which should help them to gain more control over their own life. Behaviour therapy is not, as is sometimes mistakenly believed, a treatment which can be given to people against their will. In fact quite the reverse is true. In behaviour therapy people work with the therapist, and by themselves, to try and overcome their problems, often in a gradual, step-by-step way, and their own motivation is essential.

Behaviour therapy will focus very closely on the present situation and on the upsetting symptoms and reactions that your son or daughter experiences. It will not search for the underlying reasons for their problems but will encourage the young person to learn more appropriate ways of responding that will cause them less distress. However, most therapists practising behaviour therapy will have additional skills such as counselling or psychotherapy, which they can also use, if appropriate.

The first sessions with the therapist are likely to be spent in finding out exactly what the problem is and whether behaviour therapy is likely to be helpful. Your daughter or son will probably be asked to give a detailed description of their behaviour leading up to, during and following their distress. This can help both the therapist and the young person to see more clearly how they are responding to their anxiety, what the triggers for their distress might be and how they themselves and those around them are affected by the problem. They may also be asked to keep a diary in between sessions to try and identify factors that help to increase or decrease their anxiety. Sometimes it may be suggested that they monitor their anxiety during the day to see if there is any pattern to their reactions.

If the therapist and your daughter or son decide that behaviour therapy would be helpful they will agree to work together towards a particular aim. This may be quite simple, such as being able to stroke a cat, for a young person who is terrified of cats, attending certain lessons, for someone affected by school phobia, or travelling three stops on a train, for a young person who is worried about making journeys.

The methods used in behaviour therapy may include discussion, commonsense approaches and one or more of a range of techniques, some of which are accompanied by relaxation. If relaxation is needed your daughter or son will be taught a suitable relaxation method and encouraged to practise regularly until they are able to relax quickly and easily even in difficult circumstances. Behaviour therapy also frequently involves tasks for people to carry out at home. Family or friends may be able to offer support with these.

It should be apparent whether behaviour therapy is the right approach for your son or daughter after a few sessions. If so, it is unlikely to be a very lengthy treatment. They may well achieve a satisfactory improvement with between 10 and 20 sessions, sometimes less. Sessions, which usually last an hour, may be weekly at first, with longer intervals between them as the young person gains in confidence. The fact that they are involved in planning and monitoring their own treatment, and in trying to overcome difficulties through their own efforts, can help to give them a sense of self-esteem which often spreads to other areas.

Among the more common techniques used in behaviour therapy are desensitisation and exposure treatment or flooding. Although their names are rather offputting the techniques are very straightforward.

Desensitisation
This is a technique that can be helpful with certain phobias. The young person will be asked to list specific situations related to their fear that make them anxious. For someone who is terrified of spiders these might range from, hearing a spider mentioned or seeing a picture of a spider to handling a live spider. Then, starting with the least threatening, they will gradually work through and master each situation with the help of the therapist and a relaxation technique until they overcome their fear. In some cases

they may prefer to face the situations in their imagination first before moving on to deal with them in reality.

Exposure or flooding

This technique is used to encourage the young person to confront whatever is most frightening for them, with the support of the therapist. For example, they might make a train journey, if they were frightened of trains or stand in a busy supermarket, if they were frightened of shops. At first their anxiety will mount and be very hard to handle but if they can remain in that situation for perhaps half an hour or an hour they will discover that their anxiety naturally subsides. This can be a very effective way of overcoming fear. Once they have managed the situation with a therapist they can practise with the support of family or friends until they can deal with it by themselves.

However, if such an approach seems too daunting the therapist may suggest confronting the fear but in a more gradual way. For example, if your daughter or son is frightened of crowds, they might gain confidence by learning to deal with smaller numbers of people to start with.

If your daughter or son needs help with compulsive behaviour the same technique can be used. They will be asked to put themselves in the circumstances where the compulsive behaviour takes place and refrain from carrying out their rituals for as long as possible. They will find that at first their anxiety will mount and they may need a great deal of support from the therapist or friends or family. However, the anxiety will gradually subside and they will realise that nothing dreadful occurs if the ritual is postponed or omitted. They will be encouraged and supported to gradually refrain from these rituals for increasing periods of time until they can overcome the compulsive behaviour (see Chapter 3).

COGNITIVE BEHAVIOUR THERAPY

Cognitive behaviour therapy is often helpful for certain types of depression or anxiety or where a young person lacks confidence. Despite its rather offputting name it is a straightforward and commonsense approach and one that your son or daughter can help to plan and monitor themselves. 'Cognitive', in this context, refers to the way we think about ourselves and the judgements we make about other people and situations.

When someone is distressed or lacking in self-esteem they are highly likely to view themselves in a negative light. In addition they may often misinterpret situations and other people's intentions in a way that further increases their own low opinion of themselves or adds to their distress. For example, rather than accepting that a friend has a previous arrangement, your son or daughter may believe that they are really refusing to see them that day because they no longer like them. Similarly, instead of being pleased when someone pays them a compliment, they may be convinced that the person does not mean it and is in fact laughing at them behind their back. Cognitive behaviour therapy aims to break this cycle by encouraging people to think and behave in a more flexible and positive way.

If the therapist and your son or daughter agree that cognitive behaviour therapy may be useful they will work together to identify the negative thoughts and beliefs that reinforce depression or anxiety and explore a range of alternative and more positive reactions. For example, rather than telling themselves that there is no way they can cope with a certain situation, which tends to become a self-fulfilling prophecy, your son or daughter may learn to say, 'This may make me anxious but I can probably manage if I take it slowly, step by step.' And rather than believing they must be unlikeable because they have only a few friends, they may practise stating firmly, 'I have friends who I know like me and I can probably make more friends if I wish.'

During the sessions your son or daughter should expect to have their ideas challenged and to learn how to challenge them themselves. This is to encourage them to become more flexible. For example, the therapist may ask them to list all the reasons they can think of for not attending a particular social event, and then challenge them on each of these reasons, or they may be asked to provide arguments for and against their present view of a situation. Role play or relaxation methods may be used to help young people deal with situations where they lack confidence or become highly anxious.

As a homework task they may be asked to keep a diary so that they can begin to recognise their own negative patterns of thinking and how these affect the way they view themselves and those around them. It may also help them to identify more satisfying areas of their life as well as strengths that they can draw on. The therapist may also ask them to test out negative statements in practice such as asking a friend to go to the cinema when they are sure that no one wants to see them. Should the friend by any chance refuse, then the therapist is there to offer support and explore the next positive steps that the young person can make.

It is not a lengthy form of therapy. If it proves effective then an average of about 12 one-hour sessions at intervals, with tasks to carry out at home, should enable the young person to begin to see themselves and others in a more realistic way and find useful strategies to cope.

GROUP WORK

This approach can be particularly helpful when young people who have experienced similar difficulties or where they feel more confident in a group setting. Many young people are prepared to be open and honest with their peers and to learn from each other and accept criticism in a way that they would find impossible to do with adults. A young person who resorts to silence or terse replies, when confronted by an individual therapist, is often quite responsive in a group. This may be because they feel less vulnerable and more confident when they are working alongside other young people, rather than in a one-to-one relationship with the therapist, which they may find rather threatening. Sometimes the therapist may introduce activities, as these often prove helpful in breaking the ice and encouraging communication, particularly with younger adolescents.

Groups may be held for a variety of purposes ranging from helping young people to explore the way they form relationships to looking at eating problems or learning assertion skills. Groups vary in size but there are often one or two therapists for about six to ten young people. Groups will probably meet weekly for an hour or an hour and a half, sometimes for a set period such as ten weeks and sometimes for longer. The techniques used will vary. For example, some groups will be run on counselling or psychotherapy lines and may go under the name 'group therapy', while groups that are about acquiring practical social skills may be known as 'social skills groups'. Other groups may use a variety of techniques according to the needs of the young people and the skills of the therapists concerned.

Group therapy

The young people participating will be encouraged by the therapists to share their difficulties and offer suggestions and insights to support each other. They will be expected to treat everything discussed in the group as confidential and to realise that they have a responsibility to other members of the group.

Your son or daughter can benefit through listening to what others have to say and through working through their own problems and helping other young people to work through theirs. Close relationships formed within the group may help to give them confidence in making relationships outside the group.

If your son or daughter feels anxious about the thought of talking about themselves in front of others you can reassure them that most of the group will feel like that at the start. There is no need to rush in and say a great deal until they feel comfortable. However, once members of the group start talking freely they will probably be relieved to find that many of the fears and feelings, which they thought that they alone had experienced, are in fact shared and understood by other members of the group.

The therapists may try to adopt a fairly unobtrusive role and if there are periods of silence they will not necessarily intervene. However, they will be there to ensure that the group offers a safe setting where young people can learn about themselves and where, if criticisms or suggestions for change are made, a great deal of support is given as well. Group therapy can be helpful for a wide range of problems, but if your son or daughter is very insecure then individual therapy may be more suitable

Social skills groups

Young people who are absorbed in struggling with their own difficulties may miss out on opportunities to acquire useful social skills or they may lack the confidence to practise those they already possess. Social skills groups try to remedy this situation by encouraging young people to practise social skills appropriate to their age both in the group and at home with family and friends. In some cases young people may be helped on a one-to-one basis.

Many of the skills learned focus on verbal and non-verbal communication. Although many young people are deliberately uncommunicative at times, at any rate with adults, it is important that they know how to communicate and how to make a good impression, should they wish to do so. Otherwise they may find it harder to make and keep relationships or manage in everyday situations which involve finding out or giving information, for example, or simply joining in a conversation.

Sessions are likely to include looking at the impressions people make through their body language, such as facial expressions, eye contact and gestures, and through their tone of voice and pace of speech, for example, as well as ways of initiating conversation and of listening and responding appropriately. Your daughter or son may then go on to practise situations such as telephoning to find out about a job vacancy or going for an interview. Later, with the backing of the group they may try out some of these situations in real life.

The therapist may use a variety of techniques to help young people gain in confidence. These may include demonstrating various skills, which they will then encourage the young people to practise, sometimes with the help of a video, and involving the young people in role play and in commenting on each other's performances.

Assertiveness training

Assertiveness techniques may be taught in a social skills group or a special assertiveness group. This does not mean that your son or daughter will be encouraged to become aggressive or selfish. Being assertive simply means that they have learned to accept that their own needs and feelings are important too and that they are able to express them in a calm and confident way. Assertiveness training can be very helpful for anyone with low self-esteem. Courses are also sometimes run by colleges and other organisations.

Your daughter or son will learn a number of skills through discussion, role play and other exercises to help them take more control over their own lives. For example, they might practise ways of saying 'no', politely but firmly, when they feel they are being pressured against their will; or they might practise making a request if they find it difficult to ask for anything for themselves. They may learn to give and receive criticism in the safe setting of the group and to offer compliments and receive them in a pleasant and genuine way. They will be encouraged to test out these skills in actual situations.

Some young people expect too much of themselves or try too hard to please and become very anxious as a result. Assertiveness training can help them to see that it doesn't matter if they sometimes make mistakes and that it is important to think about what they really want from life rather than trying to please others all the time.

Practical skills

Some social skills groups may include sessions on 'living skills' to help young people become more independent, or your daughter or son may attend a separate living skills or practical skills group. Such groups might discuss matters such as budgeting, dealing with social security, legal rights or the use of leisure, or they might plan a menu, do the shopping and cook a meal for example.

ARTS THERAPIES

If your son or daughter has difficulties in identifying or expressing their feelings in a verbal way or is reluctant to answer questions about themselves, they may respond well to an arts therapy approach involving art, drama, movement and dance or music therapy. These therapies are often carried out in groups but they may also be offered on a one-to-one basis.

Young people often feel safer if they can explore their emotions at one degree removed, through a painting or through improvising a story, for example. This gives them the opportunity to discover truths about themselves at their own pace and to reveal them in a way that they find easier to handle. Moreover, discussion with the therapist or with members of the group is likely to flow more easily when everyone is involved in an absorbing activity.

Although arts therapies can help people get in touch with their deeper and perhaps distressing feelings, they are often a highly enjoyable and enriching experience and this is important for those young people for whom life has become very grey and restricted.

Your daughter or son will not need any skill or ability to participate in this sort of therapy but they may well find that carrying out a particular project or exercise can give them a great sense of satisfaction. Working with these therapies can provide young people with the opportunity to explore different aspects of themselves in a safe setting and enable them to gain a clearer sense of their own identity.

Like many distressed young people your daughter or son may feel trapped in their own inner world. Encouraging them to express their individual feelings and perceptions in a creative way such as through dance or drawing, can help break down this sense of isolation. In addition, the fact that their creative efforts are accepted and treated with respect by the therapist gives value to their experiences and increases their sense of self-esteem.

Art therapy

In art therapy the young person might expect to draw, paint or make things with their hands, for example. Together with the therapist they may then use what they have created as a starting point for a discussion of their feelings.

Art tends to be a messy medium and this in itself can sometimes help young people to get back in touch with their childhood spontaneity. In addition, whatever they are creating may go wrong or they may be dissatisfied with it. The realisation that this is not the end of the world but that something can be changed or that you can start again is an important learning process for young people lacking in confidence, and one that they may be able to transfer to other areas of life.

Drama therapy

Drama therapy may involve a variety of activities such as creating characters, improvising scenes, enacting myths or stories, using props to stimulate the imagination or interpreting poems, for example. Activities such as these give young people the chance to look at their own situation and feelings from a comfortable distance and test out possible reactions in an imaginary setting. Drama therapy can also help to encourage change by giving them the opportunity to explore different sides of their personality and to experiment with different roles. Drama therapy differs from psychodrama, which tends to work more exclusively with recreating life situations and with role play.

Dance and movement therapies

Our minds and bodies closely interact in the way we experience and express emotion. However, if your son or daughter is distressed they may well be focusing on problems in their head and ignoring signals from their body. Through exploring different types of gesture and movement, these therapies enable young people to become more aware of their bodies and how they really feel and to find ways of expressing these feelings. This in turn may give them a stronger sense of their own identity and may help them to direct their energies in a more positive way in the outside world.

These therapies can also help to improve physical health and fitness and reduce stress and tension, which can be particularly helpful if your son or daughter is very anxious or depressed. Young people, who may be inhibited and self-conscious, often find that these therapies help them to begin to behave more naturally and spontaneously with other people and to feel more comfortable with their bodies and the way they look and move.

Music therapy

Young people may be able to express deep feelings through music that they are unable to communicate in words. These feelings will be picked up by the music therapist as they explore sounds together through using their voices or playing accessible instruments such as percussion, for example. By responding musically in the same mood the therapist shows that they understand these feelings, and this can help to make the young person feel accepted and valued. As a trusting relationship develops with the music therapist young people can begin to explore some of their underlying tensions and anxieties. Communicating through music in this way may help the young person to become more confident in making and sustaining relationships in the outside world.

CHAPTER 13

Drug Treatment

Whether or not the doctor suggests prescribing drugs for your son or daughter's mental health problem may depend on a number of factors including the young person's age, the type and severity of the problem, whether alternative treatments are available and the doctor's own views.

In general most doctors are reluctant to prescribe for younger adolescents, and child and adolescent psychiatrists are far less likely to offer drugs than adult psychiatrists (see Chapter 9). They usually believe that some form of talking or behaviour therapy is a more appropriate way of dealing with most young people's problems, although in a few cases, of course, medication may be advised.

These sorts of option are not so readily available to doctors treating older adolescents, as services for this age group are very sparse. GPs and adult psychiatrists are more likely to treat older adolescents as they would adults and to prescribe drugs for certain mental health problems that seem to be severe, intense or long lasting. If, after talking to the doctor, you or your son or daughter are still worried about whether this is the right treatment, you could always ask for a second opinion.

Parents are likely to be closely involved in decisions taken about the treatment of their son or daughter up to the age of 16. Beyond that age they may still have a role to play but it may be more in terms of giving advice and support to the young person (see Chapter 14).

INFORMATION

Doctors offering medication should make sure that young people and their parents, where appropriate, have the requisite information about the advantages and disadvantages of the drug concerned and an opportunity to discuss the matter so that they can make an informed decision about treatment. If this does not occur, or if you are unclear about what has been said, there is a range of questions that your daughter or son should ask, or that you should ask on their behalf.

You, or your daughter or son, will want to establish just what the aims of a particular drug treatment are. You also need to know how important the doctor considers the treatment will be in this particular instance. If the treatment is not a matter of urgency you may want to find out whether there are other alternative treatments that could be tried first.

Then you will want to know about common adverse side-effects. All drugs have some side-effects and these will have to be balanced against the distress caused by the mental health problem itself and its effects on your son or daughter's life. Some side-effects wear off gradually in the first few weeks while others may develop over time. Doctors are sometimes unwilling to discuss adverse effects as they feel it makes people even more anxious. However, it is usually less worrying to know that slight dizziness or dry mouth, for example, are due to the medication and not to a separate cause. And, of course, it may be important to establish whether the drug affects the ability to drive or do skilled tasks. You will also want to find out whether there are any risks involved in taking the drug in the long term.

Your doctor will check your son or daughter's medical history before prescribing. It is important to mention any points that may have been missed such as a suspected allergy, asthma attacks or a family history of heart disease for example. The doctor will also want to know whether they are taking any other medication. Other medication may interact adversely with the drug being prescribed, and in some cases could be dangerous, so it is best avoided unless the doctor advises that it is essential. In the same way over-the-counter drugs such as cough medicine, alcohol, and of course illicit drugs, should also be avoided while taking the prescribed drug. You may need to discuss this with your son or daughter to make sure they understand the reasons.

If drug treatment is agreed then you will want to be sure that your daughter or son has details about the drug itself. The more they know the more they can feel that they are participating in their own treatment and the more supportive you can be. It can be useful to know whether the name of the drug mentioned is the generic term (the name agreed by an international authority) or the manufacturer's brand name, and whether it belongs to a particular group of drugs such as antidepressants, for example. This information may be useful in discussing present and future treatment with other professionals or voluntary organisations, for example. The young person will need to be clear about how often the drug should be taken, whether before or after meals and what to do if a dose is missed.

Make sure you find out how long it will be before the drug is likely to have the desired effect. Some drugs take two to three weeks or even longer, although side-effects may occur more quickly. If the young person does not realise this they may give up too soon because they feel it is not helping them. It is also important to remember that drugs need to be taken regularly to take effect. You may have to find ways to remind your son or daughter without seeming to nag. You may also need to explain tactfully that they should not come off the drug or alter the dose without consulting the doctor. When they do come off a drug they usually need to do so gradually to avoid distressing withdrawal symptoms. If it is appropriate and acceptable, it may help if you take charge of the medication, keeping it in a safe place and making sure that it is taken at the right time.

Your doctor may be unable to tell the young person how long the treatment will last. Each person's situation is different and each person responds to medication in different ways. The doctor should see your daughter or son regularly to monitor the treatment but if there is any worry about side-effects or if the drug does not seem to be working in the expected way, try to persuade them to make an earlier appointment. The doctor may need to adjust the dose or switch to a different drug.

Finally, it is important to ask the doctor what other forms of support or therapy are available alongside medication. Drugs may alleviate the symptoms in certain mental health conditions, thus enabling the young person to feel less confused, anxious or depressed, for example, but they are not a magic solution. The young person and their family will still need help in sorting out any stresses that may have contributed to the problem in the first place as well as the additional difficulties caused by the problem itself, such as loss of confidence. In some cases you may have to be persistent to make sure that you get this very necessary help.

If medication is being discussed for your daughter or son you may hear one of the following drugs or group of drugs mentioned.

ANTIDEPRESSANTS

If your son or daughter has been severely depressed over a long period and counselling or other forms of support have been tried without success, the GP or psychiatrist may suggest prescribing one of a variety of antidepressant drugs. Antidepressants may also be offered if they have been very severely depressed every day for about two weeks or more, especially if there is thought to be a risk of suicide. Symptoms of severe depression may include disturbed sleep patterns, loss of appetite, loss of energy, slowed reactions or agitation, social withdrawal, feelings of guilt and worthlessness and suicidal ideas (see Chapter 4). Antidepressants will not relieve intermittent depression or general feelings of misery. They are not usually prescribed for mild depression since this usually responds better to talking and other forms of support (see Chapter 12).

Antidepressant drugs take some time to act in the body and it may be three to four weeks before the young person begins to feel better. Physical symptoms often improve first, with the young person starting to sleep more normally and regaining their appetite. Gradually they may find that they are becoming more alert and active again and have less difficulty in concentrating and remembering things. Finally their mood may improve, although they may still have the odd bad day for a time.

It is important that your son or daughter does not decide to stop taking antidepressants as soon as they feel better, as the depression may well then recur. The doctor will probably advise them to remain on antidepressants for at least a month or so longer and then to come off gradually to prevent unpleasant withdrawal symptoms.

Like all drugs, antidepressants do have side-effects, which may be apparent shortly after taking the drug and may affect different people in different ways. Adverse effects, which vary according to the antidepressant, may include drowsiness, dry mouth, constipation and blurred vision, for example. These usually diminish as treatment proceeds.

Some types of antidepressant are extremely dangerous if taken as an overdose. The doctor may decide to prescribe only a limited quantity of the drug at one visit, if there are any worries about suicide, or you may need to keep the tablets under your control.

Although antidepressants are effective in relieving severe depression in the majority of cases, they do not work for everyone.

ANTIPSYCHOTIC DRUGS

Drugs from this group, which are also known as major tranquillisers or neuroleptics, can be used to help control distressing symptoms such as hearing voices or feeling persecuted which occur when a young person is out of touch with reality as, for example, in episodes of what psychiatrists term 'schizophrenia' (see Chapter 6). They are powerful drugs which need careful monitoring and should generally be prescribed by a psychiatrist after consultation with all concerned, and as part of a general plan of treatment and support. A GP is unlikely to prescribe these for a young person except in an emergency.

It may take some days or weeks before the young person experiences improvement. Sometimes other people may be aware of their improvement first. As they start to recover the dose will probably be reduced. However, they will probably be advised to continue taking the drug for some time after they feel better to avoid the danger of a relapse and then to come off gradually. Where there is doubt about whether the young person will remember to take the drug it can be given in the form of an injection which may last from two to six weeks, or longer, providing they agree.

Among the more common adverse effects of an antipsychotic drug are drowsiness, dry mouth, blurred vision, dizziness and indigestion, but these usually diminish as treatment continues. However, there are risks of more serious adverse effects if the drug is taken continuously for several years, although this may depend on the dose taken. You will all need to weigh up these risks carefully if long-term treatment is suggested as a preventative measure for your son or daughter. It may be worth suggesting that they come off the drug if they appear to be coping, even if they have to go back on at a later stage.

Antipsychotic drugs may also be used short term to alleviate severe anxiety or episodes of mania along with other therapy.

LITHIUM

Lithium, a mineral element which is found naturally in rocks and also in very small quantities in the body, is sometimes prescribed for young people with very severe depression or to help control mild attacks of mania. It may also very occasionally be prescribed as a maintenance treatment for young people who have had several bouts of mania or mania and depression in order to try and prevent future episodes or at least reduce their severity and frequency (see Chapter 4).

Lithium does appear to be effective in stabilising mood for the majority of people diagnosed with manic depression, although it cannot help everyone. However, it does need to be administered with great care as there is only a very narrow margin between a dose which is too low to be effective and one which is high enough to be dangerous. As this varies for each person, careful monitoring is essential.

If the young person is prescribed lithium they must be sure to eat a balanced diet containing normal amounts of salt, and drink sufficient fluids. Lithium is excreted in the urine. Too little salt, or dehydration, will reduce urine flow and may cause a dangerous build-up of lithium in the body. Your son or daughter should also keep the doctor informed of any adverse effects they notice. Some of these, such as nausea, mild hand tremor or diarrhoea, can be dealt with by adjusting the dose.

Regular checks on the level of lithium in the blood are essential. It is also important for your son or daughter to be aware of the signs that lithium may have reached a dangerous level in their body. If they experience weakness, unusual clumsiness or unsteadiness on their feet, slurred speech or difficulties in thinking clearly they should stop taking lithium and contact the doctor immediately.

BETA-BLOCKERS

If your son or daughter suffers from severe anxiety with physical symptoms such as palpitations, sweating and tremor the doctor may suggest taking a beta-blocker drug which can help to reduce these symptoms and make the anxiety more manageable, perhaps during a very stressful period. The doctor should also suggest other ways of helping the young person to learn to deal with their anxiety. Beta-blockers have no effect on psychological symptoms of anxiety such as worry, tension and fear.

The doctor will probably prescribe a course for about a month starting with a low dose to see whether that is effective. The drug usually begins to work within a couple of days. Adverse effects are not usually very noticeable although some people experience a dry mouth or drowsiness. These drugs should not be taken by anyone suffering from asthma, diabetes or heart disease.

MINOR TRANQUILLISERS

Once widely prescribed for a range of anxieties, minor tranquillisers, which belong to the benzodiazepine group of drugs, are now treated with great caution. Those taking them for longer than a few weeks risk becoming dependent, and withdrawal symptoms can then be extremely distressing. However, doctors may occasionally prescribe them in very small doses for young people suffering from very severe anxiety. If so, it is important that the doctor monitors treatment and offers other support. The prescription should never be open-ended and the aim should be for the young person to come off as quickly as possible, preferably within a week or so.

CHAPTER 14
The Law and
Your Rights

Legislation involving young people and their parents covers a number of areas such as social services, health and education and is extremely complex and confusing, though there have been efforts to make some areas of the law simpler in the Children Act (see below). In addition there have been many changes in recent years both in legislation and in what is widely recommended as good practice and there are likely to be many more. Some professionals may not have fully caught up with recent changes so parents and young people may need to be particularly vigilant and seek independent advice either from another professional or an appropriate organisation or a lawyer specialising in the field (see Chapter 15).

This chapter gives a brief sketch of some of the legislation you may hear referred to and some of the most important rights of both parents and children in England and Wales at the present time. The laws and the way they operate are often very different in Scotland and Northern Ireland. Organisations which offer relevant information and advice for parents and young people in Scotland and Northern Ireland are listed in Chapter 15.

It can be quite daunting if professionals use legal terms or refer to legislation or rights that you are not familiar with. But don't hesitate to ask questions if you don't understand. There is no reason why you should be expected to know about the various Acts, orders and regulations affecting children and families. Remember too that there are various voluntary organisations that will be able to explain relevant points to you in more detail, if necessary, and advise you appropriately (see Chapter 15).

Sometimes, even when the intention behind the legislation appears excellent, there are difficulties in putting it into practice due to cuts in services. However, parents and children should not be put off and should press for their rights. Again there are various organisations that can offer advice and support (see Chapter 15).

SOCIAL SERVICES
The Children Act
One of the main purposes behind the 1989 Children Act, which covers England and Wales, is to make the law on a wide range of topics simpler, friendlier and more accessible to ordinary people. The Act brings together all the law relating to the responsibilities both of parents and the social services for the upbringing, care and protection of children, and covers matters ranging from the role of both parents in a separation or divorce to the provision of social services for families in need. It emphasises that the welfare of the child or young person must be the overriding concern when any arrangements are made and that the child's view should always be listened to and taken into account. The Act deals in the main with children up to the age of 18.

Parental responsibilities: The Act is based on the belief that it is right for children to be brought up within their own families wherever possible and that both parents have responsibilities to their children which they retain even after a divorce or when their child is being looked after by the local authority. Sometimes these responsibilities may be shared with others who are looking after the child, or curtailed by a Court Order, but they are never lost unless the child is adopted.

Working with parents: The Act encourages parents and professionals to work together to find ways of managing that safeguard

228

the well-being of the children. Legal proceedings should only be used as a last resort when all other means have been tried and then only if they are considered to be in the best interest of the child.

'In need': Under the Children Act social services have a duty to provide support and services ranging from counselling to accommodation for children 'in need' and their families. They also have a duty to work closely with relevant organisations to ensure that other appropriate services can be offered. Children 'in need' are those whose health or development appears to be adversely affected by factors such as poor living conditions, family stress or some kind of disability. Social services make an assessment to see whether the child or young person and their family qualify for such services.

As services are likely to vary greatly from area to area and resources are bound to be stretched, parents may find it useful to talk through the situation with a helpful professional or someone from an advice agency to sort out which points they want to emphasise before asking for an assessment. A supporting letter from a professional or an advice agency may also help.

Accommodation: Social services can arrange accommodation for a child or young person who is 'in need' if the parent and child wish, either in the short term to cover an emergency or longer term to enable problems to be sorted out. Accommodation might be with relatives, in a foster home or in a residential home or school, for example. Parents retain all their parental rights and responsibilities for children up to the age of 16 who are being accommodated and can take them back home whenever they wish. Young people of 16 or 17 can act independently from their parents. If they are 'in need' they can ask social services to provide accommodation for them whether or not their parents agree, and they have the right to decide whether or not they wish to return home.

Safety and protection: In most cases parents are likely to co-operate with social services on a voluntary basis. However, where this has not been possible and where social services are worried about a child or young person's safety and well-being they can step in and apply to the courts for permission to take measures that they feel may be necessary to protect the child. Depending on the situation, these might include applying for a Child Assessment Order, which means that the courts can order the parents to co-operate in a medical or psychiatric assessment of the child; for an Emergency Protection Order to remove the child to a safe place for a short period of time; or a Care Order to take the child into the care of the local authority, if it is felt the child is suffering or likely to suffer significant harm through lack of parental care or control. Parents and children have the right to appear in court and have their views heard, and to appeal against certain decisions. However the situation is so complex that they should seek advice from a solicitor on the Law Society's Children Panel or from one of the relevant organisations listed in Chapter 15.

Partnership: Even if a child is taken into care social services should still try and work in partnership with the whole family, just as they would if the child was in accommodation. All decisions, in either situation, must take into account the views of the child and parents as well as those of other friends and relatives who are important to the child. Similarly the child's race, culture, language and religion must be considered before any decisions are made. Every effort should be made by social services to enable parents, relatives and others important to the child to remain in regular contact with a child living away from home. Social services have a duty to make plans for all children they are looking after, and these plans should be regularly reviewed. Parents and children should be invited to these reviews.

Secure accommodation: Occasionally young people may be locked in a secure room in a special centre if they are thought to be a danger to themselves or others. There are strict guidelines as to the circumstances in which this may happen. Children may not be placed in secure accommodation for longer than 72 hours without a Court Order. If an application for a Court Order is made the parents will be notified. The young person must be legally represented and parents are entitled to legal representation.

Complaints: Social services must publish details of their complaints procedure. Ask social services for a copy if you have not been given one and wish to make a complaint. It may be useful to get advice from a helpful professional or voluntary organisation if things are not straightforward.

Scotland and Northern Ireland: For information and advice on the rights of young people and their families in Scotland consult the Scottish Child Law Centre or the Scottish Child and Family Alliance (see Chapter 15). In Northern Ireland there are no equivalent voluntary organisations. For information contact your local Health and Social Services Board (address in the telephone directory).

HEALTH
Consent to treatment
Although you will obviously want to find the best possible treatment or course of action for your son or daughter, you may have to accept that their view of what is best for them may differ from yours or from the professionals concerned. Young people have the right to be consulted about any treatment or other decisions involving them and they should feel confident that their views will be listened to and respected.

If your son or daughter is aged 18 or over they are considered an adult and can consent to or refuse treatment on their own behalf, irrespective of your wishes. Young people aged between

16 and 18 are also for the most part treated as adults and may expect, in the vast majority of situations, to have the same rights. However, their rights to refuse treatment may very occasionally be overridden by a court. If your son or daughter is under the age of 16 and is considered by the doctor to have 'sufficient understanding and intelligence' they can consent to their own treatment, although they may not have the same right to refuse treatment to which their parents give consent. If they are not considered to have 'sufficient understanding and intelligence' the consent of their parents or those with parental responsibility should be sought.

Consent must always be obtained from the young person or the person with parental responsibilities except in an emergency, where prompt action is essential either to save life or prevent a serious and immediate danger to the young person or to others, and except where young people are detained under certain sections of the Mental Health Act 1983 (see p. 234). This means that in very rare circumstances they can be treated without their parents' or their own consent, but this should only ever be as a last resort.

Mental health legislation

There is no mental health legislation which specifically protects the interests of young people under 18 who are admitted to a psychiatric ward or to an adolescent unit on an informal basis, although young people admitted on a formal basis (that is, detained) have the same rights under the Mental Health Act 1983 as those aged 18 and over (see p. 234). Parents and young people need to be particularly vigilant in making sure that their rights are not overlooked.

Code of Practice: The Code of Practice to the Mental Health Act 1983 does have a special section on the care and treatment of young people under 18 admitted as either informal or formal patients. Although not legally binding, the Code can be referred to as evidence in legal proceedings and any failure to follow the Code may be taken into consideration in complaints about care and treatment, including those about negligence.

The Code emphasises that young people should be kept as fully informed as possible about their care and treatment and that their wishes should always be taken fully into account. It states that wherever possible they should have the right to make their own decisions, particularly treatment decisions, and stresses that any intervention in their life should be the least restrictive possible and should result in the least possible segregation from family, friends, community and school.

Information: Parents are likely to need information and advice if their child has been admitted as either an informal or formal patient (see also Chapter 11). This may be available from a professional such as the hospital social worker, for example, or from one of the relevant organisations listed in Chapter 15. Young people can seek advice from the Children's Legal Centre or MIND. The Law Society can put parents or young people in touch with lawyers on their Mental Health Panel who have experience in advising and representing people detained under the 1983 Mental Health Act.

Informal patients: These patients, also known as voluntary patients, consent to their own admission and have the right to refuse treatment and discharge themselves if they wish. The vast majority of young people are admitted as voluntary patients but the use of the term 'voluntary' can be misleading. In practice it is usually parents, or those with parental responsibility, who make the arrangements about admission for young people under 16, although the young person should always be consulted. And although young people under 16 can consent to their own admission and treatment, as long as they are judged to have the intelligence and understanding to do so, they do not necessarily

233

have the right to refuse admission or treatment when their parents have consented, or discharge themselves against their parents' wishes. Although young people between 16 and 18 might expect to consent to or refuse admission and treatment on their own behalf, in very occasional circumstances their rights to refuse treatment may be overridden by the court.

As a parent you should make absolutely sure that your son or daughter's views are listened to by professionals and taken into account, even when their rights to make certain decisions independently from you are not clear. You also need to remember that even when your son or daughter is taking decisions independently they may still need your support to help them express their own wishes and safeguard their rights. It is also important that you make sure that professionals keep you regularly informed about your son or daughter's condition and that both you and the young person are consulted about any changes in treatment or other decisions being made. You should make sure that you never sign a form giving blanket consent for any treatment.

Formal patients: A small minority of young people will be formal patients. This means they will be detained under the Mental Health Act 1983, which covers England and Wales, but this should always be seen as a last resort. The Act outlines the grounds on which people can be detained, the various ways in which this can be carried out and the safeguards for detained patients and their rights of appeal.

The main grounds for detaining people of any age are that they are suffering from a mental disorder to such a degree that warrants detention for either assessment or treatment and that they also need to be detained in the interests of their own health or safety or for the protection of others. Detained patients are not free to leave hospital when they wish and there are special rules about treatment and whether or not they have the right to refuse it. People should be given both oral and written information on their main rights when they are admitted to hospital.

There are various ways of compulsorily detaining someone which are outlined in different sections of the Mental Health Act. Sometimes these methods are simply referred to by their appropriate section number, and a detained person may sometimes be referred to as having been 'sectioned' or being 'on a section'. There are also various ways of discharging a person who has been compulsorily detained. If you are unable to understand explanations given to you by hospital staff, your local citizens advice bureau, MIND or the Children's Legal Centre should be able to help. Lawyers on the Law Society's Mental Health Panel can also advise (see Chapter 15).

Complaints: If you or your son or daughter have a complaint about health service conditions or treatment that cannot be sorted out with the staff concerned, it should be put in writing either to the hospital manager or to the consultant in charge of the case. Making a complaint can be very complicated so do seek advice first from your local community health council or an organisation such as MIND or SANELINE in England and Wales, from the Mental Welfare Commission in Scotland and from the local Health and Social Services Board in Northern Ireland (address in telephone directory).

If your son or daughter is a detained patient in England or Wales, the Mental Health Act Commission, a body set up to protect the rights and interests of detained patients, can look into complaints once other means have been tried. In Scotland the Mental Welfare Commission deals with complaints from both detained and voluntary patients while complaints from detained patients in Northern Ireland are dealt with by the Mental Health Commission for Northern Ireland (see Chapter 15).

Scotland and Northern Ireland: For information on mental health legislation in Scotland consult the Scottish Child Law Centre, the Scottish Association for Mental Health or the Mental Welfare Commission; for Northern Ireland consult the Mental Health

Commission (see Chapter 15) or your local Health and Social Services Board (see local telephone directory).

EDUCATION

Education is compulsory up to the age of 16 and all young people, including those in hospital, are entitled to full-time education up to the age of 19, if they wish. The only exceptions are young people detained in penal institutions or under the Mental Health Act 1983.

If your daughter or son is having severe emotional problems that are affecting their schooling or their relationship with their school and you are unable to sort these out with the staff concerned, it is important to get proper advice either from a professional such as an educational psychologist or an education welfare officer (see Chapter 9), or from a relevant organisation such as the Advisory Centre for Education or the Children's Legal Centre (see Chapter 15).

Education law and practice have changed considerably in recent years and are still changing. Those advising you may well refer to legislation such as the 1981 Education Act, the 1988 Education Reform Act and the 1993 Education Act, so some relevant sections of the Acts are briefly described below.

The 1981 Education Act makes local education authorities responsible for meeting the educational needs of individual children who have difficulties in learning by ensuring that suitable resources are provided for them within ordinary schools, wherever possible, or at other appropriate schools. Young people with difficulties in learning include those with difficulties due to emotional problems.

Under the 1993 Education Act, regulations and a Code of Practice will be drawn up setting out details of procedures which must be followed when a young person is assessed for special educational needs and when a statement of those needs is prepared. Those taking part in the assessment are likely to include school staff, an educational psychologist, a doctor, and any other relevant professional who can provide information on the young person's needs, as well as the parents themselves. All those contributing to the assessment will prepare reports and the parents and the young person will have an opportunity to state their needs.

These needs will then be discussed with the local education authority and a statement will be produced which describes the young person's needs and the provision that will be made to meet these needs. Such provision might include one-to-one teaching, or extra support in the classroom, for example. If parents do not agree with the content of the statement they can appeal. The statement must be reviewed each year to monitor progress and see what changes in provision may be required. Parents should be invited to the review and details about the procedure to be followed will be provided in regulations under the 1993 Education Act.

Parents who want an assessment of their son or daughter's special education needs can write direct to the Director of Education at their local education authority. Parents who are not happy with a statement can refuse to sign and can appeal. They should ask for advice on either count from a relevant organisation such as the Advisory Centre for Education or the Children's Legal Centre(see Chapter 15).

The 1988 Education Reform Act, which enabled a National Curriculum to be brought into effect, also has provisions to enable head teachers to temporarily exempt young people from all or part of the National Curriculum due to special circumstances such as illness. Young people who have statements must have any appropriate modifications to the National Curriculum specified in their statements.

Under the 1993 Education Act schools may exclude young people for up to 15 days in any one term or permanently for serious breach of school rules. Permanent exclusion should only be carried out as a last resort. If it seems likely that your son or daughter may be permanently excluded it is important to seek advice immediately so that you understand the procedures to be followed. The effects of exclusion can be very damaging to a young person's self-esteem as well as to their education. Advice on exclusion is available from the Advisory Centre for Education (see Chapter 15).

Scotland and Northern Ireland

There is as yet no education pressure group in Northern Ireland. For information on education in Northern Ireland consult your local Education and Library Board (address in telephone directory). In Scotland consult the Scottish Parent Teacher Council (see Chapter 15).

THE CORONER'S COURT

Despite parents' anguish at discovering their son or daughter's sudden death, which may be through suicide, they will still have to complete the proper legal procedures and undergo a great deal of questioning. It will usually help if a relative or close friend can offer support in handling these very distressing matters, particularly as those closest to the young person are highly likely to be in a state of shock.

If the young person is found by their family or those who know them they can either call their GP, who will certify that they are dead and inform the police, or call the police directly who will take details and who may bring in their own police doctor to confirm the death. The CID will also be informed and a plain-clothes officer may call to inquire into the circumstances.

The police will then get in touch with the Coroner's officer, who will arrange and pay for an undertaker to take the body to the mortuary for a post-mortem examination, which is a legal requirement in this situation. If the death occurs away from home the police will try to identify the young person through property.

The CID and Coroner's office will be informed and the body taken to the mortuary, where a member of the family or someone who knows the young person well will be asked to identify them.

If the post-mortem shows that death was not from natural causes an inquest must be held. However, as the inquiries associated with the inquest will take some time to complete, the Coroner will open the inquest to issue papers to enable the funeral to go ahead. The inquest will then be adjourned, usually for a few months, to enable the Coroner's officer to gather detailed information about the young person and the circumstances of their death from their family, from doctors and from the police officers concerned, for example, and to allow time for any samples to be analysed by a laboratory.

Parents need to know that the inquest will be held in public and that the press may be present, as this can cause further distress. The Coroner will have the written information that has been prepared and is likely to question a member of the family and perhaps doctors and police who have been involved. After hearing all the evidence the Coroner will decide on one of a possible number of verdicts. For example the verdict might be that the young person has killed themselves, or an open verdict may be given if it is thought that the young person may not have been fully aware of the consequences of their action. If the death is the result of some form of drug abuse a verdict of accidental death might be recorded. Once the verdict has been reached the death can be registered and the family can obtain a copy of the death certificate.

Scotland and Northern Ireland

Procedures are similar in Northern Ireland. In Scotland there is no similar procedure but in certain circumstances a Fatal Accident Inquiry may be held. For further details contact your local Procurator Fiscal (address in the telephone directory).

CHAPTER 15

Other Sources
of Help

This chapter describes some of the organisations that can offer information, advice or support or refer you or your son or daughter to other appropriate sources of help. It is by no means comprehensive but is intended as a useful starting point. Most of the organisations listed have a national office that you can contact or a network of local offices or groups. In addition you may also find that there are other useful local organisations or groups in your area. Ask at your local library, citizens advice bureau or community health council (see below).

Some organisations are staffed by paid staff, some by volunteers and some by a mixture of both. Depending on the organisation, you should expect those you come in contact with to have had some training or personal experience in that particular field. They should be able to offer information, advice or support in a language that is clear, jargon free and easy to understand and in a non-judgmental way. If for any reason you are not happy with the response you receive, ask whether you might speak to someone else.

You may wish to contact such an organisation for information or advice or to talk to someone who will understand your anxieties and who will not dismiss your worries as simply fussing. Talking things over with a sympathetic outsider may help you sort out what the problem is and give you the confidence to press for professional help if necessary. Although some organisations are set up specifically for young people or parents, most of them will try and offer some help to other members of the family or to friends who are concerned.

Help offered by organisations such as those listed is usually free and confidential but if you have any doubts do check first. Please send a large stamped addressed envelope if you are requesting information as most organisations operate on very tight budgets. Some may offer free booklets and factsheets while others may charge. Many will have a suggested reading list for those who want further information.

One advantage of this kind of help is that there is usually a quick response once you contact the organisation. You should not have to wait weeks to talk to someone or to receive the information you need. However, some organisations may only operate restricted hours and staff may be very stretched. Try to be polite and patient, but be persistent too. It is important to get the right information and advice.

Most organisations now have answering machines for out-of-hours calls or for when staff are at meetings or away from the office. It can sometimes be disconcerting to get a recorded message when you have just plucked up courage to make a call. It might help to think before you telephone whether you wish to leave a message or would rather try again.

Telephone helplines

There has been an increase in the number of telephone helplines in recent years. You or your daughter or son may sometimes find it easier to talk about worries or problems to someone on a helpline who has been trained to listen over the telephone. This can be particularly helpful if it is the first time that you have been able to admit that there is a problem, or that support is needed because things seem to be getting out of hand.

Quite often it is easier to be frank if you cannot see the other person and do not have to give your name. Another advantage is that you can make the call at the time you choose; you do not

have to travel, make an appointment or wait in unfamiliar surroundings.

Helplines operate in a variety of ways. Some offer support by
listening and being there in a crisis; others may encourage you to
talk through problems in order to help you decide what steps to
take. Some will also offer information and suggest other services.
Talking to someone who understands may help you to feel calmer
and less isolated and to see things in a different light.

Freefone lines and 0800 numbers will not appear on itemised
phone bills. However, other calls may. If this is likely to cause a
problem you may prefer to use the phone of a trusted friend or
relative.

GENERAL SOURCES OF HELP
Citizens Advice Bureau (CAB)
Trained CAB workers offer information and advice on a wide
range of topics such as benefits, housing, debts, employment and
legal problems as well as family and personal difficulties. They
can also assist in practical ways, for example with filling in forms,
writing letters or making complaints. The service is free and confidential. Your CAB should have details of local services and
helpful national and local organisations, including support
groups and counselling agencies. Some CABs have a solicitor
available at certain sessions to give free advice.

Anyone can use a CAB but, depending on local arrangements,
you may need to make an appointment or you may be able to call
in and wait your turn. Opening times vary, so check on these
first. Some CABs will give advice over the telephone but lines
tend to be very busy and you may find it hard to get through. To
find your nearest CAB look in the telephone book under 'citizens'
or ask at your local library.

Community Health Councils (CHCs)

Your local CHC is there to represent your interests in the health service. Contact them to find out about NHS services for adolescents in your area and for advice if you are experiencing difficulty with any aspect of the health service or if you wish to make a complaint. They should also have information on services provided by the local authority and voluntary organisations and on self-help and support groups. There is usually one CHC in each health district. It will be listed in the telephone book under 'community' or under the name of your local district health authority.

In Scotland Local Health Councils serve very much the same function although they do not advise on making complaints. In Northern Ireland advice on services and on voluntary organisations is available from the local Health and Social Services Board (address in the local telephone directory).

Ethnic communities

If you belong to a closely-knit ethnic community it may help to discuss your anxieties with someone from your community whom you trust and who understands the particular stresses that you and your son or daughter are experiencing. Such a person may be able to suggest appropriate sources of help within the community or acceptable courses of action.

Local advice agencies

There may be advice centres in your area offering advice on a range of topics, rather like a citizens advice bureau (see above), or specialising in areas such as law or benefits, for example. They may be able to help you or point you in the right direction. To find out what is available ask at your town hall or library.

Places of religious worship

If religion plays an important part in your life then there may well be someone sympathetic at your place of worship who has experience of young people's problems and who is skilled at listening. It may be helpful for you to discuss your worries with them or for your son or daughter to talk to them in confidence. Many religious organisations also offer support such as counselling and practical assistance. Never feel embarrassed to ask what is available.

Private care

If you have private health insurance for your family it may be possible for your son or daughter to see a psychiatrist privately for a consultation and perhaps treatment. However, they must be referred by their GP to a consultant psychiatrist and you should always check first with your insurers to find out whether there is cover. Private medical insurance is unlikely to offer cover for psychotherapy. If you are paying out of your own pocket you can make your own arrangements, providing your son or daughter agrees, though it is always sensible to discuss this with the GP and to ask about charges first.

Your son or daughter is not likely to be offered different or better treatment privately, but they are likely to be seen more quickly and in more comfortable surroundings. They will also be seen each time by the consultant psychiatrist and not by a junior doctor.

To find the name of a private educational psychologist in your area ask your local education authority (the address will be in the telephone directory under the name of your local authority). To find the name of a private clinical psychologist in your area contact the

> British Psychological Society
> St Andrew's House
> 49 Princes Road East

Leicester CE1 7DR
Tel: 0533 549568

For private counselling or psychotherapy contact the British Association of Counselling (see p. 250); for private psychotherapy contact the United Kingdom Council for Psychotherapy (see entry on p. 250).

Probation service

If you are worried about your daughter or son's activities and afraid that they may be breaking the law, you can telephone the duty officer of your local probation service in England, Wales and Northern Ireland to discuss your worries, anonymously if you wish. The address should be in the phone book under 'probation service'. The duty officer may be able to offer advice and support or may suggest that you talk to a probation officer specialising in juvenile offenders. All probation officers are trained social workers. However, if the young person is under 16 it may be more appropriate to contact the duty officer at your local social services department. In Scotland you should contact your local social work department.

If a young person is found guilty of an offence at a youth court the probation officer or social worker will see the young person and their family to prepare a pre-sentence report. It is important that any stresses or mental health difficulties should be discussed so that they can be taken into account.

Public libraries

Your local library is a good place to find out about the resources available in your area. The librarians should be able to provide information about local services, local and national voluntary organisations, support groups, classes, clubs and recreational activities, or point you in the right direction. They can also help you find books or other information relating to the difficulties affecting your child.

Schools

Young people who are stressed or anxious may behave differently at home and at school. It is important to have good contact with your child's teachers so that everyone is aware of any difficulties at an early stage. Parents and teachers can then work together with the young person to try and sort out any problems. The school may have its own sources of help or be able to suggest other agencies. If you know that your child is particularly upset, perhaps because of a divorce or bereavement, be sure to let the school know so that allowances can be made. Don't wait till the end of term to talk over any worries. Contact the form teacher, head of year or head teacher and ask if you can come in as soon as possible and talk in confidence about your child.

Social services

A parent or young person can contact their social services department to ask for information on services for adolescents in their area. They can also ask to see the social worker on duty in their area to talk over problems. Depending on the situation the social worker may suggest other helpful organisations or services or may offer further help from social services. Social services are listed in the phone book under the name of your local authority.

SPECIALISED SOURCES OF HELP
Abuse

NSPCC Child Protection Helpline
If you know that a young person is being abused or your are worried about the possibility of abuse you can phone this helpline run

by the National Society for the Prevention of Cruelty to Children, to talk to a trained social worker. You do not have to give your name. They will listen to your worries and advise you on what steps to take. If necessary they will also pass on the details to an appropriate agency to ensure that the young person is properly protected. Young people who have been abused can also telephone for help and for referral to appropriate agencies if they wish. The helpline offers a 24-hour service every day of the year for callers in England, Wales and Northern Ireland. Calls are free and will not appear on an itemised telephone bill.

Call: 0800 800 500

Scotland does not have a similar 24-hour helpline. If you want to talk over any worries and what to do in confidence you can telephone your nearest RSSPCC (Royal Scottish Society for the Prevention of Cruelty to Children) office during working hours (look in your telephone directory for the number or ask at your library or CAB).

PAIN. Parents Against INjustice
This organisation offers advice, counselling and support to parents and young people in England and Wales when a child is mistakenly thought to be at risk or to have been abused. It also offers support to parents in Scotland and Northern Ireland. Publications available. Write or telephone the advice line between 10 a.m. and 4 a.m. weekdays.

> Parents Against INjustice
> 3 Riverside Business Park
> Stansted
> Essex CM24 8PL
> *Tel:* 0279 647171

Alcohol problems

Al-Anon and Alateen
If you are worried that your son or daughter may be drinking too much you can ring Al-Anon's 24-hour confidential helpline to talk things through. Al-Anon also has a network of family groups throughout the UK offering support and information to relatives and friends of people who have drinking problems. Alateen, which is part of Al-Anon, offers support to teenagers who have friends or relatives with a drinking problem.

For information on your nearest local groups and for the helpline contact:

> Al-Anon Family Groups
> 61 Great Dover Street
> London SE1 4YF
> *Tel:* 071 403 0888

Alcohol Concern
Parents or young people can write for information on all alcohol problems. Alcohol Concern will send leaflets and details of local services in England and Wales, where appropriate.

> Alcohol Concern
> 275 Gray's Inn Road
> London WC1X 8QF
> *Tel:* 071 833 3471

In Scotland contact the Scottish Council on Alcohol, which also provides free counselling for young people and their families.

> The Scottish Council on Alcohol
> 137–145 Sauchiehall Street
> Glasgow G2 3EW
> *Tel:* 041 333 9677

In Northern Ireland contact:

> Council on Alcohol
> 40 Elmwood Avenue
> Belfast BT9 6AZ
> Tel: 0232 664434

Bereavement

Cruse–Bereavement Care

This organisation offers information, advice and counselling to all bereaved people either directly or through local branches throughout the UK where these exist. If someone close to your son or daughter has died you could contact Cruse for advice or suggest that they contact Cruse themselves. Anyone wishing to speak directly to a bereavement counsellor can telephone the Cruse–Bereavement line weekdays between 9.30 a.m. and 5 p.m. Leaflets and other literature are available. Telephone or write to:

> Cruse–Bereavement Care
> Cruse House
> 126 Sheen Road
> Richmond
> Surrey TW9 1UR
> *Tel*: 081 940 4818

> *Cruse–Bereavement line*: 081 332 7227

The Compassionate Friends

Parents who have suffered the death of a child of any age can contact this organisation, which offers befriending and support through a self-help network of parents across the UK. Publications available. Parents and families of children who have ended their lives can gain support from a group within the Compassionate Friends known as 'Shadow of Suicide'. Telephone or write to:

TCF National Office
53 North Street
Bristol BS3 1EN
Tel: 0272 539 639

Bullying

The Anti Bullying Campaign

Parents and young people can write or telephone between 9.30 a.m. and 5 p.m. weekdays to talk to advisers who have personal experience as a parent of a child who has been bullied or of being bullied themselves and who can offer support and advice on what steps to take. Publications.

The Anti Bullying Campaign
10 Borough High Street
London SE1 9QQ
Tel: 071 378 1446

Counselling

British Association for Counselling (BAC)

You may find you need some counselling or therapy yourself to cope with problems thrown up by your son or daughter's difficulties, or you may wish to find a counsellor or therapist for them. The BAC can send you a list of counsellors and counselling and psychotherapy organisations in your area, together with details of training, qualifications, specialisation and fees. Details of free and low-cost counselling, where this exists, are also given. Write, enclosing an A5 stamped addressed envelope, to:

British Association for Counselling
1 Regent Place
Rugby CV21 2PJ

United Kingdom Council for Psychotherapy

The Council serves as an umbrella for a large number of psychotherapy organisations in the UK. Practitioners in these organisations must be trained and qualified to certain standards and abide by a specific code of practice and ethics. The Council does not refer people to psychotherapists directly but can put you in touch with appropriate member organisations such as the Association of Child Psychotherapists or the Institute of Family Therapy, who can in turn tell you of the nearest practitioner in your area should you or your son or daughter wish to see a psychotherapist privately. Be sure to check on fees first as these can vary widely.

> United Kingdom Council for Psychotherapy
> Regent's College
> Inner Circle
> Regent's Park
> London NW1 4NS
> *Tel*: 071 487 7554

Youth Access

This is the umbrella organisation for youth counselling, advice and information centres throughout the UK. Help at these centres is usually free and always confidential. The aim of Youth Access is to support young people through their difficulties and enable them to take control of their own lives. You or your son or daughter can contact Youth Access to find out if there is an appropriate agency in your area. They do not offer counselling or advice themselves. Telephone or write for details to:

> Youth Access
> Magazine Business Centre
> 11 Newarke Street
> Leicester LE1 5SS
> *Tel*: 0533 558763

Crisis lines

Childline

Children or young people who are worried or at risk can ring this free telephone helpline from anywhere in the UK to talk to a trained volunteer counsellor in confidence. Counsellors listen and offer support to young people experiencing a wide range of problems including physical and sexual abuse, bullying, sexual and relationship difficulties and suicidal feelings. They can suggest – other sources of help. They will only get in touch with social services or the police with the young person's permission.

The lines are open every day 24 hours a day, but the caller may have difficulty in getting through and need to be persistent. This number will not show up on itemised phone bills. The Childline number is: 0800 1111.

If they prefer they can write (no stamp needed) to:

> Childline
> Freepost 1111
> London N1 0BR

Samaritans

Samaritans provide a completely confidential 24-hour telephone service seven days a week. They are there to listen to your pain and distress without making judgements or offering their own solutions. If you are feeling very worried about your child and do not know where to turn, it may be a relief just to talk to someone about your innermost feelings. Young people too may find it easier to disclose their true anxieties in confidence to someone over the telephone who will not be shocked by what they hear. You can also drop in at most Samaritan centres during the day and evening. Samaritans will also accept calls from another person on behalf of a young person who wants to make contact. They will then normally get in touch with them by telephone. Your local Samaritans will be listed in the phone book.

SANELINE

Parents or young people can telephone SANELINE to talk to trained volunteers who offer information and support on serious mental health problems. They can also put them in touch with local organisations and services throughout the UK. The line is open from 2 p.m. to midnight every day of the year. Leaflets are available. SANELINE is run by the charity SANE, which campaigns to improve conditions for people with serious mental illnesses and their families.

> SANE
> 2nd Floor
> 199–205 Old Marylebone Road
> London NW1 5QP
> *SANELINE*: 071 724 8000

Drug problems

ADFAM National

Families of drug users anywhere in the UK can contact this organisation for support and for information about drugs and details of services for families and drug users. Leaflets available. Write or telephone the helpline between 10 a.m. and 5 p.m. weekdays.

> ADFAM National
> 1st Floor, Chapel House
> 18 Hatton Place
> London EC1N 8ND
> *Tel*: 071 405 3923

Families Anonymous

If you are worried about your son or daughter's use of drugs and how to cope with it you can ring this helpline which is run by volunteers who have been through similar situations and who will understand your anxiety. Free leaflets available. You may also wish to join a self-help group to give you support if there is one in your area. Contact:

Families Anonymous
Room 8, 650 Holloway Road
London N19 3NU
Tel: 071 281 8889

Freefone Drug Problems

To find out what services are available you can dial 100 and ask the operator for Freefone Drug Problems. A recorded message will give you a telephone contact for your area who can tell you about local services. Contact numbers are available for counties in England and for Wales, Scotland and Northern Ireland.

Institute for the Study of Drug Dependency

This organisation provides information on all aspects of drug taking. They can give you information over the telephone or send you leaflets, or more detailed information, if required. There may be a charge for written material. They do not give advice.

Institute for the Study of Drug Dependency
1 Hatton Place
London EC1N 8ND
Tel: 071 430 1993

Narcotics Anonymous (NA)

If your son or daughter has a problem with drugs and wants to do something about it you might suggest they contact this self-help organisation to see if there are meetings in your area. The can write, or telephone between 10 a.m. and 8 p.m., 7 days a week for information on local meetings. All calls are answered by drug-free recovering addicts who will understand their worries.

Narcotics Anonymous
PO Box 1980
London N19 3LS
Tel: 071 498 9005

Release

Drug users or their friends or family can contact this drug and legal advice 24-hour telephone helpline from anywhere in the UK. They will be able to speak in confidence to a drug counsellor or solicitor during office hours or to a trained volunteer out of hours. Release can advise on the effects of both illegal and prescribed drug use and on legal problems associated with drugs. They can also provide details of local welfare and support agencies and of local solicitors who are experienced in this field. Anxious parents are welcome to write or telephone. Leaflets available.

> Release
> 388 Old Street
> London EC1V 9LT
> *Tel*: 071 729 9904
> *out of hours*: 071 603 8654

SCODA (The Standing Conference on Drug Abuse)

If you are worried that your child may be developing a drug problem you can ring or write to SCODA for general advice and for information on local services throughout the UK. Your son or daughter can also contact them for advice and information.

> SCODA
> 1–4 Hamilton Place
> London EC1 8ND
> *Tel*: 071 430 2341

For information on services in Scotland you can also write or telephone:

> Scottish Drugs Forum
> 266 Clyde Street
> Glasgow G1 4JH
> *Tel*: 041 221 1175

Eating problems

Eating Disorders Association (EDA)

Parents or young people can telephone to talk in confidence to someone who understands the problems of anorexia, bulimia and compulsive overeating. The helpline is open from 9 a.m. to 6.30 p.m. weekdays. There is also a youth helpline for young people aged 18 and under, on Monday, Tuesday and Wednesday from 4 p.m. to 6 p.m. If you join the EDA you will receive free publications and be put in touch with local self-help groups and services where these exist. Contact:

> The Eating Disorders Association
> Sackville Place
> 44–48 Magdalen Street
> Norwich, Norfolk NR3 1JE
> *Tel*: 0603 621414
> *Youth helpline*: 0603 765050

Education

Advisory Centre for Education (ACE)

This organisation offers information, advice and support on educational problems to parents with children in state schools. Young people can also contact them. Write or telephone. The advice line is open on weekdays between 2 p.m. and 5 p.m. Publications available.

> Advisory Centre for Education
> 1B Aberdeen Studios
> 22–24 Highbury Grove
> London N5 2EA
> *Tel*: 071 354 8321

CSIE (The Centre for Studies on Integration in Education)
Parents and young people in England and Wales are welcome to
contact CSIE for advice on the 1993 Education Act and integration in state schools.

>CSIE
>415 Edgware Road
>London NW2 6NB
>*Tel*: 081 452 8642

There are no equivalent organisations in Scotland. General advice
and suggestions on where to go for help may be obtained from

>Scottish Parent Teacher Council
>Cramond House
>Cramond Glebe Road
>Edinburgh EH4 6N5
>*Tel*: 031 312 3062

There are no equivalent organisations in Northern Ireland at present.

Foster care

National Foster Care Association
If you are a foster carer anywhere in the UK you can contact this
organisation for information, advice and support. They may be
able to put you in touch with a local group. Publications and
training courses available. Telephone or write to:

>National Foster Care Association
>Leonard House
>5–7 Marshalsea Road
>London SE1 1EP
>*Tel*: 071 828 6266

HIV and AIDS

National AIDS Helpline

Parents of young people can telephone this confidential helpline free of charge from anywhere in the UK. It is open every day 24 hours a day. Trained advisers offer information and advice on HIV, AIDS and safer sex and suggest other appropriate services and agencies. Calls do not appear on itemised bills. Special helpline services are available in both English and other languages (Cantonese, Mandarin, Punjabi, Bengali, Hindi, Urdu, Gujerati and Arabic) at certain times. Ring the main helpline for details on 0800 567123.

Terrence Higgins Trust

Parents or young people can contact this charity for information, advice and help on any aspect of HIV or AIDS. They can phone the helpline and talk through worries with a trained counsellor who will offer support and suggest appropriate services, if necessary, or they can write for free leaflets. The helpline is open from noon to 10 p.m. every day of the year.

> The Terrence Higgins Trust
> 52–54 Grays Inn Road
> London WC1X 8JU
> *Helpline*: 071 242 1000

In care

Family Rights Group

You can contact this organisation, which covers England and Wales, for information and free independent advice if you have a child in care or if you are involved in child protection procedures. They may be able to help you directly or put you in touch with other organisations or a local group or contact. Publications available. Write or telephone for information. For advice phone the advice line on Monday or Friday from 9.30 a.m. to 12 p.m. or on Wednesday between 1.30 p.m. and 4 p.m.

> Family Rights Group
> The Print House
> 18 Ashwin Street
> London E8 3DL
> *Tel*: 071 923 2628
> *Advice line*: 071 249 0008

In Scotland contact the Scottish Child and Family Alliance who will put you in touch with appropriate organisations.

> Scottish Child and Family Alliance
> 5 Shandwick Place
> Edinburgh EH2 4RG
> *Tel*: 031 228 8484

In Northern Ireland contact Child Care (NI) who will put you in touch with appropriate organisations.

> Child Care (NI)
> 2A Windsor Road
> Belfast BT9 7FQ
> *Tel*: 0232 234499

NAYPIC (National Association of Young People in Care)
Young people who are in care or who have been in care in England and Wales can contact this organisation for information and advice on how to obtain their rights. Publications available. The organisation is run by young people who have been in care themselves. Telephone or write to:

> NAYPIC
> 8a Stucley Place
> London NW1 8NJ
> *Tel*: 071 284 4793

In Scotland contact

Who Cares? Scotland
The Templeton Business Centre
Block 1, Unit C1
Glasgow G40 1BA
Tel: 041 554 4452

Legal

Children's Legal Centre

Young people can contact this organisation for information and advice on any aspect of law and policy affecting children and young people in England and Wales. Parents can also use the service on behalf of the young person. Publications available. Write or telephone the advice line between 2 p.m. and 5 p.m. weekdays:

The Children's Legal Centre
20 Compton Terrace
London N1 2UN
Tel: 071 359 9392 (publications)
Advice line: 071 359 6251

In Scotland contact

The Scottish Child Law Centre
Lion Chambers
170 Hope Street
Glasgow G2 2TU
Tel: 041 333 9305
Freefone service for under-18s: 0800 317500

There is no equivalent organisation in Northern Ireland.

Law Society

The Law Society can put parents or young people in England and Wales in touch with local lawyers on their Children Panel who have specialist knowledge of legal proceedings affecting young people under the 1989 Children Act and who can advise them of their rights. They can also put them in touch with local lawyers on the Mental Health Panel who have specialist knowledge of the 1983 Mental Health Act. Contact:

> Law Society
> Administrator, Children Panel or Mental Health Panel
> Ipsley Court
> Barrington Close
> Redditch
> Worcs B98 0BR
> *Tel*: 0527 517141 *or* 071 242 1222

Lesbian and gay

Acceptance
Parents can write or telephone the helpline to talk through their feelings about having a gay son or lesbian daughter with someone who will understand. The helpline is open from Tuesday to Friday from 7 p.m. to 9 p.m. but you can try during the day, if necessary. Newsletter and other literature available.

> Acceptance
> 64 Holmside Avenue
> Halfway Houses
> Sheerness
> Kent ME12 3EY
> *Tel*: 0795 661463

London Lesbian and Gay Switchboard
This 24-hour confidential advice and information helpline is staffed by trained volunteers who are themselves lesbian or gay. Young people can phone for a chat and to discuss concerns which may include sexual preferences, safer sex and difficulties with family or friends. They can obtain details of local youth

organisations for lesbian and gay people and local helplines throughout the UK, where these exist. Parents are also welcome to ring.

Tel: 071 837 7324

Mental health commissions

Mental Health Act Commission

If your son or daughter is a detained patient in England or Wales and has a complaint about their care and treatment that cannot be sorted out through the usual channels they can contact the Commission or you can contact them on their behalf:

> Mental Health Act Commission
> Maid Marian House
> Houndsgate
> Nottingham NG1 6BG
> *Tel*: 0602 504040

Mental Welfare Commission for Scotland

Young people, whether they are detained or voluntary patients, can contact the Commission if they have a complaint about their care or about their treatment for a mental health problem which they cannot sort out through the usual channels, or you can contact the Commission on their behalf. The Commission can also provide general information on mental health matters or point people in the right direction.

> Mental Welfare Commission
> 25 Drumsheugh Gardens
> Edinburgh EH3 7RB
> *Tel*: 031 225 7034

Mental Health Commission for Northern Ireland

If you or your daughter or son have been unsuccessful in pursuing a complaint about their care or treatment for a mental health problem either in hospital or in the community, with the appropriate health and social services board, you can write giving details to the Mental Health Act Commission. The Commission can also give general information on mental health matters or point people towards helpful organisations.

> Mental Health Commission
> Elizabeth House
> 116–118 Holywood Road
> Belfast BT4 1NY
> *Tel*: 0232 651157

Mental health organisations

Manic Depression Fellowship
You can contact this self-help organisation for sufferers and relatives for information about manic depression and for details of local self-help groups in England, Scotland and Wales.

> Manic Depression Fellowship
> 13 Rosslyn Road
> Twickenham
> Middlesex TW1 2AR
> *Tel*: 081 892 2811

MIND. National Association for Mental Health
MIND campaigns for better mental health services in England and Wales through its national head office, its regional offices and network of affiliated local groups. It aims to uphold the rights of people with mental health problems and increase public understanding. You can write or telephone national MIND for advice and information on mental health. Contact the Information Unit if you want information. For legal or welfare rights problems contact the Legal and Parliamentary Unit, preferably by letter. MIND also publishes a range of books and leaflets.

Contact National MIND for the address of your regional

MIND or local group, or look in the telephone book. Both your regional MIND and your local group should be able to give you information on useful services in your area.

National MIND
Granta House
15–19 Broadway
London E15 4BQ
Tel: 081 519 2122

Scottish Association for Mental Health (SAMH)
SAMH is the Scottish equivalent of MIND and has the same broad aims. You can write or telephone (weekdays 9.30 a.m. to 12.30 p.m.) for general information on mental health matters and details of local services.

Scottish Association for Mental Health
Atlantic House
38 Gardeners Crescent
Edinburgh EH3 8DP
Tel: 031 229 9687

Northern Ireland Association for Mental Health (NIAMH)
NIAMH is the Northern Ireland equivalent of MIND and has the same broad aims. You can write or telephone for general advice on mental health matters and details of local services. Young people aged 17 and over may be able to attend one of the mental health resource centres run by NIAMH for therapy and recreation, or join a self-help group. Contact:

Northern Ireland Association for Mental Health
80 University Street
Belfast BT7 1HE
Tel: 0232 328474

NSF
You can write or telephone the NSF (formerly the National Schizophrenia Fellowship) for information, advice and support

on schizophrenia and related problems. NSF produces a range of leaflets and other publications and can put you in touch with a local NSF self-help group if you wish. You can also telephone the advice line to speak to an advice worker on weekdays from 10 a.m. to 3 p.m.

NSF
28 Castle Street
Kingston-upon-Thames KT1 1SS
Tel: 081 547 3937 (for information)
Advice line: 081 974 6814

NSF (Scotland)
40 Shandwick Place
Edinburgh EH2 4RT
Tel: 031 226 2025

NSF (Northern Ireland)
Regional Office
37–39 Queen Street
Belfast BT1 6EA
Tel: 0232 248006

Young Minds
This organisation campaigns to improve mental health services and resources for children and young people throughout the UK. You can write or telephone them for information on national and local services for young people and their families. Funding permitting, a national telephone helpline for adults concerned about young people's feelings or behaviour will open in 1994.

Young Minds
22A Boston Place
London NW1 6ER
Tel: 071 724 7262

One-parent families

Gingerbread
Bringing up children on your own can be rewarding but it can also sometimes be lonely and stressful. Gingerbread is an association for one-parent families. It has a large network of self-help groups, which offer information, support and an opportunity to enjoy family activities with others. For the telephone number of a contact for your nearest local group in England and Wales write or telephone:

>Gingerbread
>35 Wellington Street
>London WC2E 7BN
>*Tel*: 071 240 0953

In Northern Ireland contact:

>Gingerbread Northern Ireland
>169 University Street
>Belfast BT7 1HR
>*Tel*: 0232 231 417

In Scotland contact:

>Gingerbread Scotland
>Community Central Hall
>304 Maryhill Street
>Glasgow G20 7YE
>*Tel*: 041 353 0953

National Council for One-Parent Families
The Council produces a number of useful free publications on topics ranging from divorce to child support. It also operates a referral service to helpful local organisations and support groups in England, Wales and Northern Ireland. Write or telephone:

National Council for One-Parent Families
255 Kentish Town Road
London NW5 2LX
Tel: 071 267 1361

In Scotland contact:
The Scottish Council for Single Parents
13 Gayfield Square
Edinburgh EH1 3NX
Tel: 031 556 3899

Parent support

Exploring Parenthood

If you telephone this organisation from anywhere in the UK, they can arrange for a professional counsellor to call you back at a convenient time, usually within three to five days. The counsellor can help you talk through your anxieties and find you details of local services, if appropriate. There is no charge. Young people can also phone, although this is primarily a parent line. This is not a crisis service and counsellors are not immediately available as they have other jobs. Parents can also have up to three face-to-face counselling sessions in London charged on a sliding scale according to means. Letters are answered, and leaflets are available.

Exploring Parenthood
Latimer Education Centre
24 Freston Road
London W10 6TT
Tel: 081 960 1678

Parentline: Organisations for Parents Under Stress

Parentline volunteers work in groups to offer helpline services in different areas. At present there are groups in England and

Northern Ireland. All volunteers are parents themselves who have been trained to listen and offer support for a wide range of problems. They may also be able to suggest other services if appropriate. Parents can call when there is a crisis or when they just feel the need to talk. Helpline services operate at different times. To find your nearest helpline contact:

> Parentline
> Rayfa House
> 57 Hart Road
> Thundersley
> Essex SS7 3PD
> *Tel*: 0268 757007

or look up Parentline in your local telephone directory.

Parent Network

If you are worried about your role as a parent and the way you communicate with your child, you might find it helpful to attend a parent-link group to discuss family relationships and ways of coping. Groups usually meet weekly for 12 weeks. There may be a fee. Groups can offer support but are not a substitute for professional help, where this is needed. For details of groups, which are at present run in England, Scotland and Wales, contact:

> Parent Network
> 44–46 Caversham Road
> London NW5 2D5
> *Tel*: 071 485 8535

Parents Anonymous London

You can ring this telephone helpline to speak to a trained volunteer who also has experience in bringing up children. Volunteers will listen and offer support to parents to help them sort out their worries and decide what steps they wish to take. Callers can ring from anywhere in the UK; they simply have to pay the cost of the call. The helpline is open every day of the year from 7 p.m. to midnight and usually for some hours during the day on weekdays. An answering-machine message will give you the phone number of a volunteer to contact that day.

> Parents Anonymous London
> 6 Manor Gardens
> London N7 6LA
> *Tel*: 071 263 8918

Research

Trust for the Study of Adolescence
This organisation carries out research and training in the field of adolescence and encourages professional and public understanding in this area. It produces publications for parents and teenagers and a series of tapes to help parents cope with adolescent problems. It also produces a national directory of services for pregnant teenagers and young parents. For information contact:

> Trust for the Study of Adolescence
> 23 New Road
> Brighton BN1 1WZ
> *Tel*: 0273 693311

Running away

Missing Persons Bureau Helpline
If you are worried because your son or daughter is missing you can ring this national 24-hour helpline to talk through the situation. They will offer support and practical advice and will arrange publicity if you wish or suggest ways in which you can do so. If the young person is found but does not wish to get in contact with you directly for the time being, they can pass on messages.

> *Telephone helpline*: 081 392 2000

Sexual and relationship problems

Brook Advisory Centres
Centres welcome young people and provide confidential contraceptive advice and counselling for relationship difficulties and emotional and sexual problems. Details of local centres in England, Scotland and Northern Ireland can be obtained from the central office. Parents are also welcome to phone to find out more about the services offered. A recorded information line on 071 617 8000 gives information and details of helpful services.

> Central Office
> Brook Advisory Centres
> 153A East Street
> London SE17 2SD
> *Tel*: 071 708 1234

Smoking

Quitline. Helping Smokers to Quit
Anyone can ring this helpline, which is staffed by trained counsellors, to discuss worries about smoking and difficulties in giving up. Counsellors will offer advice and provide addresses of local 'stop smoking' groups and other useful services. It is open weekdays 9.30 a.m. to 5.30 p.m. A helpline tape is available each day out of hours.

> *Tel*: 071 487 3000

Solvent abuse

Re-Solv. The Society for the Prevention of Solvent and Volatile Substance Abuse
Parents or young people can write or telephone for information and advice on all aspects of solvent and volatile substance abuse.

Re-Solv can put you in touch with your nearest liaison worker, if one exists. Leaflets and other publications available.

> Re-Solv
> 30A High Street
> Stone
> Staffs ST15 8AW
> *Tel*: 0785 817885

Stepfamilies

Stepfamily. The National Stepfamily Association
If you are a parent, step-parent or young person in a step-family you can telephone or write to this organisation for information, advice and support. Publications available. There are some local support groups. The telephone helpline can put you in touch with qualified counsellors who take calls on weekdays from 2 p.m. to 5 p.m. and from 7 p.m. to 10 p.m.

> Stepfamily. The National Stepfamily Association
> 72 Willesden Lane
> London NW6 7TA
> *Tel*: 071 372 0844 (information and publications)
> *Counselling helpline*: 071 372 0848

INDEX

Private care, 171–72, 206, 244–45
Probation service, 245
Problems, parent's own, 37–38, 95, 202
Professionals: consulting, 167–68; differing views, 168–69: and minorities, 170; questions asked, 185–89; second opinion, 169, 193, 219
Psychiatrist, 174–76, 193–96
Psychologist: clinical, 181–82; educational, 182–83
Psychotherapist, 179; psychotherapy, 204–6
Public library, 245–46

Race, *see* minority groups
Reality, out of touch with, 123–34, 223–24, helpful organisations, 252, 263–65
Relationship, with young person: changes in, 2; difficulties, 152–54
Research, into adolescence, 269
Residential homes, 196–98
Responsibilities, 8, 13
Rights, insist on, 4, 169, 228, 232, 234
Risk taking, 14–15, 64–72
Rituals, 91–92, 117, 209
Rudeness, 15
Running away, 49–50; helpful organisation, 269

Safety, 13–14, 16, 64, 141–42, 230
Schizophrenia, 124–34, 138, 140, 223–24; helpful organisations, 253, 263–65
School: difficulties at, 29–30, 34, 51–52, 182–84;, 236–38; 246; exclusion, 237–38; new,

11–12; refusal, 90–91, 207; residential, 196–98; helpful organisations, 256–57
Secure accommodation, 230–31
Separation, of parents, 52–55
Services: press for, 164, 166, 228; confusion, 165–66
Sex: development, 9; helpful organisation, 270; relationships, 55–6
Sexual abuse, 56–61, 171, helpful organisations, 246–47, 251–52
Siblings, support for, 37, 132, 141–42, 147–48
Smoking, 64–67; helpful organisation, 270
Social phobia, 89
Social services, 180–81, 227–31, 246
Social skills groups, 213–14
Social worker, 180–81, 245, 246
Solvent abuse, 64–66, 70–72; helpful organisation, 270–71
Special needs, young people with, 31–33
State of world, worries about, 61–62
Stepfamilies, 62–64, helpful organisation, 271
Stigma, overcoming, 81
Substance misuse, 64–72
Suicide: attempted 137–39, 196; completed, 139–40, 238–39; fears about, 135, 171, 222; helpful organisations, 249–50, 251–53, 263–65; reactions to 141–43; talking about, 136–37
Support for parents, 147, 158, 163–64; helpful organisations, 267–69